Threat Perceptions

Issues in Crime and Justice

Series Editor

Gregg Barak, Eastern Michigan University

As we embark upon the twentieth-first century, the meanings of crime continue to evolve and our approaches to justice are in flux. The contributions to this series focus their attention on crime and justice as well as on crime control and prevention in the context of a dynamically changing legal order. Across the series, there are books that consider the full range of crime and criminality and that engage a diverse set of topics related to the formal and informal workings of the administration of criminal justice. In an age of globalization, crime and criminality are no longer confined, if they ever were, to the boundaries of single nation-states. As a consequence, while many books in the series will address crime and justice in the United States, the scope of these books will accommodate a global perspective and they will consider such eminently global issues such as slavery, terrorism, or punishment. Books in the series are written to be used as supplements in standard undergraduate and graduate courses in criminology and criminal justice and related courses in sociology. Some of the standard courses in these areas include: introduction to criminal justice, introduction to law enforcement, introduction to corrections, juvenile justice, crime and delinquency, criminal law, white collar, corporate, and organized crime.

TITLES IN SERIES:

Effigy: Images of Capital Defendants, by Allison Cotton
Perverts and Predators: The Making of Sexual Offending Laws, by Laura J. Zilney and Lisa Anne Zilney
The Prisoners' World: Portraits of Convicts Caught in the Incarceration Binge, by William Tregea and Marjorie Larmour
Racial Profiling: Research, Racism, Resistance, by Karen S. Glover
State Criminality: The Crime of All Crimes, by Dawn L. Rothe
Punishment for Sale: Private Prisons and Big Business, by Donna Selman and Paul Leighton
Forensic Science in Court: Challenges in the Twenty-first Century, by Donald E. Shelton
Threat Perceptions: The Policing of Dangers from Eugenics to the War on Terrorism, by Saran Ghatak
Gendered Justice: Intimate Partner Violence and the Criminal Justice System, by Venessa Garcia and Patrick McManimon

Threat Perceptions

The Policing of Dangers from Eugenics to the War on Terrorism

Saran Ghatak

LEXINGTON BOOKS
A division of
ROWMAN & LITTLEFIELD PUBLISHERS, INC.
Lanham • Boulder • New York • Toronto • Plymouth, UK

Published by Lexington Books
A division of Rowman & Littlefield Publishers, Inc.
A wholly owned subsidiary of The Rowman & Littlefield Publishing Group, Inc.
4501 Forbes Boulevard, Suite 200, Lanham, Maryland 20706
http://www.lexingtonbooks.com

Estover Road, Plymouth PL6 7PY, United Kingdom

British Library Cataloguing in Publication Information Available

Library of Congress Cataloging-in-Publication Data
Ghatak, Saran, 1973–
Threat perceptions : the policing of dangers from eugenics to the war on terrorism / Saran Ghatak.
p. cm. — (Issues in crime & justice)
Includes bibliographical references and index.
ISBN 978-0-7391-2957-9 (cloth : alk. paper) — ISBN 978-0-7391-5110-5 (electronic)
1. Crime prevention—United States—History. 2. Threat (Psychology)—History. I. Title.
HV7432.G46 2011
364.40973—dc22 2010032092

™ The paper used in this publication meets the minimum requirements of American National Standard for Information Sciences—Permanence of Paper for Printed Library Materials, ANSI/NISO Z39.48-1992.

Printed in the United States of America

Contents

Acknowledgments

I have incurred the debt, intellectual or otherwise, of many people while writing this book. This would not have been written without the encouragement of Gregg Barak, whose criticisms and advice have been invaluable throughout the process. I also thank Michael Sisskin, the editor at Lexington Books, for his help and patience. Part of the research was conducted when I received a grant from Rockefeller Archive Center. My intellectual debt to my professors—Craig Calhoun, Troy Duster, Neil Brenner, Steven Lukes, Prasanta Ray, and Veena Das—far transcends the scope of this work. I have also been fortunate enough to work with a wonderful group of colleagues at Keene State College. Special thanks goes to Peter Stevenson for being an exemplary friend and collaborator. This is also a good opportunity to say what is generally left unsaid and acknowledge my family members. Lipi Ghatak gets thanked for everything—without her almost nothing in my life would have been possible. Maitreya Ghatak, the other and better sociologist in the family, had taught me more than he realized. Maitreesh Ghatak has always provided a role model though his is a tough act to follow. Prabhati Mukherjee would have been very happy to see the completion of this book. Others—Sujoy Singh, Manishita Das, Disha Ghatak, and Darya Ghatak—complete the full circle. The faults are, of course, all mine.

This book is dedicated to all my grandparents.

Introduction

In his analysis of the development of capitalism and modern rationality in Europe, Max Weber identified capital accounting, or techniques of assessment and prediction of future gains, as one of the crucial inventions of capitalism that has shaped the contours of the Western culture (Weber 2007 [1927], 275).[1] Capital accounting or, more specifically, the techniques of double-entry bookkeeping that developed in early modern Italy allowed for quantification and calculation of profitability and capital accumulation and provided the rationality of capital investment and expansion of business enterprises. Many historians and social scientists of the era supported Weber's claim. Werner Sombart argued that capitalism is defined by rational and systematic pursuit of profit, and there is no better representation of this than the practices of bookkeeping (Sombart 1915). As Schumpeter saw it, capitalism reinvents money as much more than a currency of exchange by turning it into "a tool of rational cost-profit calculations, of which the towering monument is double entry bookkeeping" (Schumpeter 1942, 123). While money or exchange of commodities have existed for many millennia before the dawn of the modern era, the uniqueness of the capitalist culture rests on its ability to use money as a means of rational calculation that renders the future assessable and therefore predictable. This future directedness defines the quintessence of modern rationality. The ethos of calculation, assessment, and prediction of future possibilities are the hallmarks of the culture of modernity. Mathematical and statistical predictive tools have not only been central to the functioning of the market and industry but also an essential part of social and political governance in our time.

Historical scholarship has shown how the development of the first actuarial tables of calculating risk in marine trade influenced the fortunes of incipient commercial insurance industry and consequently shaped the course of mercantile capitalism in the seventeenth and eighteenth centuries (Poovey 1998). For those early generations of entrepreneurs, accounting and actuarial practices represented something far more important than simply keeping a check on expense and profit (Carruthers and Espeland 1991). It was the state of art in science of prediction that rendered the future visible and facilitated the expansion of business by calculating future profit and assessing possible risks to investment. These demonstrated the potential of objective scientific thinking and the limits of providence at the dawn of the era of secularization and disenchantment of social life. With the decline of the divine came the new sciences that sought to decipher the deeper laws of nature and to impose some order on the potentially chaotic consequences of human action. This presaged the development of the forms of knowledge that would offer some answers to the quest for controlling destiny by knowing the future. "Taming of chance," as Ian Hacking argues, is a hallmark of modern culture (Hacking 1990).

The salience of the techniques of analyzing and managing social risks in our times is built on a similar need for the ability to rationally calculate and control the possibility of future dangers, hazards and threats. Sometimes these risks are unwarranted consequences of technological and economic development, sometimes these risks come from natural mishaps, and in some cases these risks stem from human action in all its capriciousness. As some of these pose a serious threat to the functioning of the society, the art of governance of contemporary societies involves the adoption of various techniques of assessing and managing these on the basis of scientific knowledge as well as legislative and regulatory mechanisms of various kinds.

RISK AND SOCIAL THEORY

Risk has emerged as a nodal concept in sociology in recent times. Following the pioneering works of Ulrich Beck (1992) and Mary Douglas (Douglas and Wildavsky 1982; Douglas 1992), there is a burgeoning literature on the vicissitudes of the so-called risk society. In one of the most prominent analysis of the centrality of risk in contemporary social life, Beck argued that the threats of environmental and social hazards that came with modernization have become the defining feature of late modern societies. Class societies have given the way to the new epoch of "risk societies." In an earlier epoch, the problems of distribution of wealth and managing industrial conflict defined the politics and economy of capitalist industrialism. In a similar way, contemporary advanced industrialized societies are preoccupied with the problem of assessing and managing the risks emerging from the operations of the technological- industrial complex that drives the economy of these societies (Beck 1992). While revolutions in technology have freed people from the scourge of scarcity and poverty, these have also produced a series of unintended consequences that threaten the prosperity and the very survival of these societies. The problems of managing the potential or actual hazards stemming from the deployment of new technologies are more salient than questions about the redistribution of wealth and class struggle (Beck 1992, 19–20).

In a similar way, Anthony Giddens asserts that while the processes of rationalization and secularization of post-Enlightenment Western societies led to the decline of conceptions of fate and fortune, it also gave rise to an increasing preoccupation with risk or the wider consequences of human action in society. Thus understanding, calculating and ultimately managing risk is a part of the project of "colonization of the future" that comes from inherent reflexivity of the modern cultures that seeks to predict and control the possible adverse effects of human decisions in almost all fields of social life (Giddens 1991).

Beck has emphasized the real nature of the threats posed by unrestrained technological and industrial development, and the management of these environmental, technological or epidemiological hazards in his analysis.[2] However, other scholars have taken a more constructivist perspective by highlighting the importance of the cultural construction of risk perceptions. In their analysis of debates over environmental dangers, Douglas and Wildavsky argued that existing patterns of group identity and cultural outlooks have a profound effect on the ways risks are understood by competing groups and interests in society, and shape the ways debates and struggles over technological developments take place (Douglas and Wildavsky 1982). Douglas criticized the methodological individualism inherent in the rational choice theory and social psychological perspectives in the analysis of risk perception in claiming that these tend to ignore the broader cultural factors, especially the collective discussions and deliberations between citizens that shape their views on hazards that threaten their ways of life (Douglas 1997).

This work takes a similar perspective in analyzing the historical processes of construction of danger/ risk of crime in modern societies. Historically, crime has been one of the most enduring sources of risk to members of all societies. The very term implies a violation of a conduct norm, and consequently the threat of distress or harm, whether material or emotional, to a person or a collectivity. Not surprisingly, the control of crime and maintenance of law and order have traditionally been a core problematic of government from the very beginning of organized social life regardless of the variations in the forms of government and hence, techniques of achieving those ends.

RISK AND CRIME

Strategies of identification, assessment and control of risks have been identified as one of the principle operational principle in the criminal justice system over the last few decades (Ericson and Haggerty 1997; Feeley and Simon 1992; 1994; Kempf-Leonard and Peterson 2000; O'Malley 1992, 2000, 2002; Stenson 2001; Sullivan 2001). Risk management techniques used by enforcement, prosecution, and judicial institutions directed at the prevention of recidivism or future crime through various penal and judicial measures have increasingly become common. Indeed,

Simon has claimed that crime control measures have emerged as a key problematic of governance of late modern societies, and various technologies of risk management have figured very prominently in the agenda of the enforcement, judicial and correctional apparatuses of the state (Simon 2005b). The governance of contemporary society is marked by a preoccupation with proactive, preemptive, and preventive measures of neutralizing threats (Castel 1991).

The early twentieth-century tradition of crime control policies were based on the assumption that crime as a social problem could be eliminated through appropriate law enforcement measures, and offenders could be reclaimed as productive citizens through rehabilitative penal policies (Stenson 2001). Contemporary crime control policy reflects a more realist perspective that gives up on the goal of solving the problem of crime and reform offenders. Rather, there has been a movement toward controlling or eliminating potential threats of crime or minimizing harm through extensive surveillance and monitoring of criminogenic risks and likely offenders (Ericson and Haggerty 1997; Lilly 1992). At the judicial level, the traditional rehabilitative goals of penal sanctions are increasingly being supplanted by identification of likely threats or recidivists through actuarial methods and selective incapacitation through mandatory sentences. Scholars have pointed out that the development of a "managerial" approach to crime control emphasizing the administrative principles of managing the risk of crime, rather than traditional goals of reform and rehabilitation of offenders, animates the operational logic of contemporary criminal justice institutions (Feeley and Simon 1992, 1994; Garland 1996; McLaughlin and Murji 2001; Sasson 2000).

The contemporary salience of risk management is also related to the rise of the ideology of privatization. Some argue that the politics of neoliberalism in advanced industrialized nations over the last several decades rejects the state centered social insurance model that characterized the heydays of the welfare state. It is replaced by the insurance-based doctrine of "prudentialism" that seeks to make individuals responsible for controlling risks to their lives and property (O'Malley 1992, 2004). In some cases, the responsibility of security is devolved to multiple sites and institutions in society, including state agencies, private organizations, local communities, and individual citizens themselves (Ericson 2007; Stenson and Edwards 2001). Shearing and Stenning identifies the rise of a new ideology of "instrumental disciplinarity" that shifts the burden of responsibility of security against threats to private institutions. This is rooted in the ideology of cost-benefit analysis of the private sector rather than moral discourse of laws (Shearing and Stenning 1997).

The ascendance of the ideology of risk management in the criminal justice system has given rise to controversies for a number of reasons. Some have argued that the current risk prediction instruments are not accurate or infallible, and a criminal justice system that is predicated on potential rather than actual crime goes against the due process ideal of justice in democratic societies (Hudson 2003). Most importantly, these may result in extensive racial and ethnic profiling and a wide range of violations of civil liberties and constitutional rights of the citizens, as well as coercive control of the poor in societies that have grown more and more unequal over time (Sullivan 2001; Wacquant 2008; Young 1999).

The advent of risk management strategies is complemented by the equally powerful trend of harsh punitiveness and a martial rhetoric against crime (Garland 2001; Hudson 2003; Simon 1998). These developments need to be understood in the backdrop of the wider social, economic and political transformations in advanced industrialized nations over the last few decades. With the decline of the welfare state institutions, and the rise of free-market neoliberal ideology in the economy, the polity creates the conditions for the advent of a justice system predicated on risk management. Since the 1970s, deindustrialization, unemployment, and underemployment resulted in growing polarization between classes, and a rapid decay of inner cities in a number of nations. Since the 1980s, a growing consensus regarding being "tough on crime" and the consequent campaigns against crime and drugs disproportionately targeted the racialized underclass (Sullivan 2001). Along with this, growing fear of crime and the sensationalized media portrayal of the threat of violent crime contributed to growing popular support for the ideology of zero-tolerance policing, along with toughened sentencing guidelines and other penal measures to contain the risk of crime (Hollway and Jefferson 1997; Reiner et al. 2000; Stanko 2000; Walklate 2001).

While these works in the sociological/criminological literature on risk management have done much to advance our understanding of the origin and the development of these techniques, there are some areas that require more scholarly attention. Most of these tend to take the origin of these techniques as a given, and spend little time on understanding the processes that goes into the construction of the problem of risk. The discussion of risk management without investigating these processes can only lead to a very partial approximation of the nature of the problem. Risk is a dynamic category, and shaped through the intersection of cultural, scientific, and juridical processes (Maurutto and Hannah-Moffat 2006; O'Malley 2004). Also, while much of the analytical attention is focused on understanding the vicissitudes of risk management techniques in contemporary times, there is little analysis of the history and development of these practices. Risk management may have become an overt ethos of governance in recent times but this does not imply that these did not exist in the past. Indeed, as a more historically informed study of the American criminal justice system would show that the roots of the present policies could be traced back to much earlier time in history.

This work makes two specific contributions to the literature on risk, security, and crime control. First, it is premised on the idea that the very conception of risk is not a preexisting reality, but a result of simultaneous processes of social, juridical, and scientific construction. The measurement of risk in the criminal justice and the security apparatuses refer to the potential rather than an actual act, though present and past behavior are seen as predictors of the future. The processes of "dangerization" create a discourse of suspicion of people deemed to be a threat to others in society (Lianos and Douglas 2000). Risk is a legal concept, and legislations and judicial precedents institutionalize the calculation and control of risk by the criminal justice and security apparatuses of a nation. Very importantly, prediction of risk is established by scientific discourses and practices, as psychological profiles, statistical models, and other measures of risk factors renders the future calculable, hence predictable. Thus a comprehensive analysis of risk management and security practices would not be complete without a clear focus on all the processes that essentially renders an invisible reality a basis of public policy and governmental processes. Thereby analytical attention needs to be focused on the ways conceptions of crime, security, and risk has been rearticulated through the course of the twentieth century.

Second, in order to understand the current policies it is important to situate these in a broader historical perspective. While indeed the practices of risk management are more prevalent in contemporary times, the rationality of controlling or eliminating potential risks is not necessarily new in history (Pratt 1997; Rigakos and Hadden 2001; Simon 2005a). Specific aspects of contemporary risk management techniques were present in certain early twentieth-century crime control policies. Some of the earliest instances were the defective delinquency laws directed at controlling the so-called feebleminded people. Similarly, the policing of political dissent in the early twentieth century contained elements of techniques that have been revised and expanded in the contemporary era of the PATRIOT Act. The governance of risk is an intrinsic part of the criminal justice system of modern societies, and it is important to see how the different constructions of risk have informed the adaptation of different techniques of social control throughout the twentieth century.

This study adopts the perspective that Michel Foucault has called a "history of the present" (Foucault 1979). Historical knowledge in this case is not just an exercise in uncovering facts about the past. Rather, the purpose of historical knowledge in this context is to show the tortuous ways in which certain ideas and concepts about criminality and social control have developed and influenced those of the contemporary times. At the same time, it does not seek to trace a single unbroken line between the past and the present, but to highlight the conditions of emergence of these concepts and their mutability across time and space. Understanding the dispersions and divergences between the various iterations of the concept of criminal danger, and the social conditions that have produced these is necessary to make sense of contemporary ideas and debates about risk in the criminal justice system. In order to critically assess the scientific, legal, and political ramifications of contemporary risk assessment techniques it is essential to see how past history weighs on the present, for unless we understand the former we may indeed be condemned to repeat them.

The first chapter of the book outlines the early history of scientific knowledge on dangerous offenders. Two distinct discourses in the nineteenth century posited the existence of intrinsic traits of deviance that have shaped subsequent theorization of dangerousness. Criminal anthropology and eugenic theories of deviance combined evolutionary biology with the emergent sciences of anthropometry and statistics to posit the existence of innate criminality caused by developmental atavism and consequent lack of intelligence and moral consciousness. However, the emergent psychiatric discourse on crime, posited "moral insanity" as the major source of criminal danger, and the emergence of psychiatric institutions in the early nineteenth century led to some of the first theorization of criminal insanity or psychopathology.

The second chapter analyzes the eugenic theories of criminal danger in the early twentieth-century United States. While theories of hereditary defects emerged at the second half of the twentieth century, they received strong support from the eugenic movement in the first decades of the twentieth century. Francis Galton's pioneering work on anthropometry shaped the emergence of the eugenic movement in the early twentieth century. Eugenicists popularized conceptions of inherited "feeblemindedness" and related delinquent traits, and devised standardized intelligence tests to measure risk potential. Principles of social engineering inherent in eugenic thought, and its popularity led to a number of legislations to control the so-called feebleminded or "defective delinquents" in many states. The emergence of eugenic jurisprudence marks the origin of the influence of scientific expertise in general and psychiatry in particular in the criminal justice system.

The third chapter analyzes the rise of the concept of psychopathology in the early twentieth-century America. While the eugenic movement and the defective delinquency laws championed heritable cognitive disabilities as a major trait for criminal risk, the 1920s witnessed a new generation of psychiatrists who argued for acquired psychopathology as the preeminent source of criminal risk. Certain states passed "sexual psychopathy" laws that sought to incapacitate people convicted of crimes stemming from supposed pathologies of the mind.

The fourth chapter examines the conception of actuarial justice. While the application of scientific methods of measuring future risk potential is not new in the criminal justice system, contemporary practices of "actuarial justice" differ from past practices in both their scientific basis and legal ramifications. These rely on standardized statistical instruments for measuring risk potential, rather than individualized psychiatric evaluations. Many have called the efficacy of these instruments into question. These measures also represent a tension between democratic rights and public safety in the criminal justice system. Rather than rehabilitating individuals convicted of an actual offense, these seek to incapacitate potential threats to public safety through a variety of measures including preventive detention, pretrial confinement, civil commitment, and mandatory maximum sentencing. This chapter analyzes the scientific and legal controversies surrounding the emergence of actuarial practices in the criminal justice system.

The fifth chapter surveys the history of surveillance and control of political dissent through the late nineteenth and twentieth centuries. Many in the contemporary corporate and governmental circles perceived the emergence of labor activism, and left-wing political organizations as a serious threat to the American democracy. The consequent measures of suppression, both legal and extralegal, have affected the developmental trajectory of American politics and security policies.

The sixth chapter analyzes the governmental response to the threat of terrorism. The attacks of September 11 have reshaped the strategic imperatives of the security and law enforcement apparatuses in America. Traditional crime-fighting strategies are being complemented by a host of strategies aimed at a new threat to the public order. While there is a strong consensus about the strategic necessity of confronting terrorism, most of the tactical aspects of managing terror-related risk are controversial because of the conflict between concerns for democratic freedoms and national security. This chapter analyzes the transformation of the risk discourse along with the measures of containing the threat of terror by the security apparatuses of the government.

The concluding section ties together the central arguments of the book—that is, the processes of constructing risk and the historical development of risk management techniques. It argues that criminal risks or security threats are produced by interrelated discourses of political-legal and scientific institutions and practices. These are contingent constructs that are relative to a time period and the prevailing social trends. Certain technologies of managing risk or danger were inherent in the processes of governing of modern societies throughout the twentieth century, and some of these have become more prevalent over the last three decades. The disillusionment with the "rehabilitative ideal" in penal institutions at the backdrop of the wars on crime and drugs, growing public "fear of crime," and the emergence of the threat of terrorism at the new millennium have combined to legitimize more invasive techniques of law enforcement.

NOTES

1. In spite of his prescience about the vagaries of capitalism, Weber did not foresee the creative misuse of accounting norms by Enron or the recklessness of derivative traders, which have come to define the culture of business in our times.

2. Beck has argued later that the dichotomy between the constructivist and the realist perspective is a false dichotomy. Rather, the focus should be on both the actual and potential hazards as well as their construction and representation in social discourse (Beck 1999, 134).

ONE

Science and Criminal Danger in the Nineteenth Century

The very idea of risk presupposes a possibility, rather than the actuality of events or human behavior. When it comes to criminal behavior this involves the identification of criminogenic predispositions or "danger" inherent within certain people which makes them a perceived threat to public order. This conception of danger is built on a series of indices that seek to measure the potential of an individual or a collective actor to endanger other individuals. Before the development of the scientific discourse on crime, the idea of dangerousness was underlined by moral and religious conceptions within a community (Douglas 1966). The concept took a new form and importance with the rise of the scientific approaches to study crime in nineteenth-century Europe. The newly developing behavioral sciences developed conceptions of "natural" criminals whose danger lay not in action, but in the potential threat that they posed to others because of some inherited or acquired mental conditions.

The social changes associated with the industrial revolution resulted in a tremendous amount of prosperity to a section of the population. Yet a sense of security was elusive as the very existence of the teeming ranks of urban poor in the crowded tenements was seen as a threat to peace and prosperity of the cities. Contemporary observers often portrayed these neighborhoods as chancres of the body social, where deviance and delinquency of all sorts thrived and threatened to spread to the rest of the city. There arose the conception of the "dangerous class," comprising the unemployed, the indigent, the vagrant, and the "undeserving poor" of the metropolises (Brace 1872). The task of controlling this social danger became an imperative for efficient urban governance. An offshoot of these efforts was an eager embrace of specific scientific models of criminal danger constructed by contemporary scientists.

SCIENCE, DANGER, AND SOCIAL CONTROL

Some of the first scientific studies in criminal behavior were influenced by the institutionalization of the collection of quantitative data by various European governments in the early nineteenth century. Many of these early statistical studies represented an effort to search for patterns and laws of human behavior, as the availability of aggregate social statistics allowed for calculations and comparisons over time and space. Studies in "moral statistics" pioneered by Francis d'Ivernois and André Michel Guerry identified stable patterns in numbers of crime that were influenced by social conditions (Meitzen and Falkner 1891). Some of the most famous early statistical studies on crime came from the Belgian mathematician Lambert-Adolphe Jacques Quetelet. These were based on the statistics on crime collected by the French Ministry of Justice and showed the existence of patterns of regularities in the rate of crime across time and space, as well as the impact of social variables such as age, education, economic status, nationality, and gender on social behavior (Morrison 1892; Quetelet 1968 [1842]; Radzinowicz 1965). Quetelet's conclusions dealt a blow to the methodological individualism inherent in classical philosophy and jurisprudence in arguing that human behavior is determined to a very large extent by social forces rather than being true expressions of free will.[1]

While Quetelet pioneered the use of statistics in the study of society and thereby blazed the path for latter generations of social scientists, his later writings on crime were marked by a strong trend of biological determinism. He postulated that a specific deviant group marked by lack of moral judgment and depravity committed a significant amount of crime in the society (Beirne 1993). He used a disease metaphor in explaining crime and argued that criminal danger is a determined condition inherent in the psyche of specific people who are naturally predisposed to breaking laws. In one of his last works, *Anthropométrie* (1871), he championed phrenological methods pioneered by Franz Joseph Gall and Johann Gaspar Spurzheim, and posited that the natural criminals are marked by physiological abnormalities. In Quetelet's view, the task of the government was to control the danger of social disorganization by constant vigilance against this class of incorrigibles, and at the same time embark on a mission of social reform that would encourage average law-abiding citizens to flourish.

The seeds of biological determinism found in the later works of Quetelet will find a much fuller expression in the works of the so-called school of positivist criminology that emerged in late nineteenth-century Italy (Beirne 1993; Lombroso 1911 [1899]; Lombroso-Ferrero 1972 [1921]; Parmalee 1908; Rafter 1997a). Cesare Lombroso's theory of innate criminality stemming from moral and psychological atavism manifested in physiognomical anomalies drew inspiration from both Darwinian biology as well as the emergent discourses of phrenology and anthropometry. Lombroso's ideas were extended by his students in Italy, and later by Ernest Hooton in the United States (Ferri 1901, 1917 [1883]; Garofalo 1914 [1885]; Hooton 1939a, 1939b; Rafter 2004a). Criminal anthropology enjoyed a significant amount of fame for its promise to be able to prepare an exhaustive index of physical and physiognomical features that predict delinquent behavior. However, some criminologists challenged some of its conceptual and methodological premises especially the emphasis on the presence of physical stigmata, while retaining the substantive focus on the heritability of criminal behavior since the early twentieth century.

One of the most important challenges to Lombroso's theory came from an English doctor, Charles Goring, who set out to put the premises of criminal anthropology to an empirical test. Using statistical methods pioneered by the likes of Quetelet and Karl Pearson, Goring studied the records of thousands of inmates in British penitentiaries in order to examine the degree to which physiological traits could be used to predict criminality. He compared this with a control sample drawn from enlisted soldiers in a unit of the British army and college students. While his analysis showed that there are certain differences in height and weight between criminals and noncriminals, Goring did not find any substantial evidence of physical stigmata that Lombroso identified as an essential proof of behavioral and physical atavism in his sample (Goring 1913).

There was little doubt about the scientificity of his methods given that Goring based his study on a large sample and used rigorous statistical methods. Therefore critics of criminal anthropology seized this study as a conclusive rebuttal of Lombrosianism. However, closer examination of Goring's study shows that while he refutes the claim that congenital physiological markers predict criminality, he did argue that mental constitutional factors, such as defective intelligence, are an important feature in the etiology of crime. This was already posited by some of Lombroso's students. Enrico Ferri argued that along with physical abnormalities, psychological deficiencies, or what he called "moral insensibility" (often manifested in the use of slang, secret symbols, and handwriting of offenders), determine the presence of congenital criminal traits (Ferri 1901). Raffaele Garofalo asserted that "moral instincts" are not products of individual choice. Rather, these are created by evolution in a race of people, and transferred across generations. However, these might be corrupted by disease, psychological infirmities and evolutionary atavism within individuals that lead to criminal behavior (Garofalo 1914 [1885], 7). In a later period, the American anthropologist Ernest Hooton criticized the lack of scientificity in Lombroso's methods while making a strong case on the link between physical characteristics, mental abnormalities, and criminal behavior based on his study of sixteen thousand prison inmates in ten states of the United States (Hooton 1939a, 1939b).

Criminal anthropology was a part of a new approach to issues of crime and law that was known as the positivist school of criminology and jurisprudence (Beirne 1993; Garland 1985). The positivist approach was marked by a core belief that social deviance is a product of inherent pathologies of the individual transgressor and that a proper science of crime can establish an inventory of such pathological conditions and thereby predict and control delinquent behavior. This conception of criminal behavior was directly tied to a reaction against the doctrine of free will and humane punishment that underlined classical jurisprudence exemplified by the works of Cesare Beccaria and Jeremy Bentham (Foucualt 1990; Pasquino 1991; Rafter 1997a). Understanding of crime and punishment in classical jurisprudence hinged on the idea that humans are capable of making moral choices, and the breaking of a law or convention stems from a conscious decision that weighed the pleasure and pains of the consequences of one's action. Therefore the decision to commit a crime does not come from any innate condition. Rather, it is based on free will of the people and the strength of the laws lies in their capacity of deterring people from making the "wrong" decision. Both Beccaria and Bentham advocated the legislation of a system of proportional punishment that would naturally promote the virtue of abiding laws, as the pains of punishment would outweigh the possible pleasure or profit of committing an offense. The ideals of classical jurisprudence are enshrined in the legal practices of contemporary Western democracies, especially in the idea of *actus reus*, or the actual criminal offense being the fundamental substantive principle of criminal law.

Writing at the end the nineteenth century, one of the most prominent advocates of the positivist school, Enrico Ferri, led the charge against what he saw as well meaning but ineffective penal principles of classical jurisprudence. Ferri asserted that a major motivation of classical jurisprudence influenced by Enlightenment philosophies was to lessen the ferocity of punishment prevalent in Europe since the classical antiquity. He hailed the success of these ideas in bringing the institutions and practices of law enforcement in tune with civilized sentiments of modern democracies. However, he argued that while punishment had become more humane, it had not become more effective in reducing crime in society. This was due to a fundamental misconception in classical jurisprudence that failed to recognize that only a small group of people committed the majority of crimes in society. These offenders did not choose their respective courses of action by exercising moral judgment. Rather, they committed crimes because they lacked the very capacity of moral judgment due to certain innate physiological and psychological abnormalities.

Following Lombroso's work, Ferri made a distinction between "natural" and "occasional" criminals, the latter being those who committed offenses due to situational conditions or transitory temptations that overcame their moral judgment. Criminal law based on the principles of classical jurisprudence only applied to the latter group since their moral sensibilities might prevail over temptation through the knowledge of the penal consequences of their actions. However, the classical school was incorrect in its central assumption that crime simply was an infraction of law, rather than a form of natural behavior stemming from innate anomalies in certain types of humans, according to Ferri. As a result, this doctrine simply allowed harm to befall innocent people by failing to stop these innate criminals from committing an offense in the first place. Ferri advocated that criminal justice should be restructured according to scientific principles in which the "incorrigibles" whose crimes stemmed from hereditary organic, and psychological degeneracy would be identified, isolated, and incarcerated before they actually broke a law or harmed someone. Their criminality stemmed from the potential danger they posed to the society, and not always from their overt behavior. Ferri argued that criminal trials were as much clinical exercises as legal ones. A criminal judge therefore should be well versed in the principles of anthropology, psychology, and statistical procedures, as the purpose of criminal trials was not to judge the offender on the basis of the magnitude of the offense committed, but on the basis of her or his personality and threat potential. Consequently, punishment was not calibrated to the amount of harm caused by the offense, but to the remedial measures needed in order to treat or incapacitate the offender based on the level of dangerousness.

Similarly Garofalo argued that the ultimate purpose of law in a civilized society was the protection of citizens, and the existence of "natural criminals" necessitated the rethinking of criminal law and penology. He argued that identification of this category of criminal was a scientific task of great importance that should not be hindered by procedural aspects of law enforcement. The so-called natural criminals were a threat to the society since they lacked any sense of empathy for fellow humans, and they also lacked the basic moral probity necessary for civilized life. As their criminality stemmed from hereditary moral and psychological deficiencies, they could not be treated as the same as other individuals, and required a special form of justice. As many of these heritable abnormalities could not be treated or rectified, reform or rehabilitation could not be the objectives of criminal law. They could only be incapacitated by being interned for life in special penal colonies (Garofalo 1914 [1885]).

Phrenology and other anthropometrical methods posited the existence of stigmata and other physiological abnormalities as indicators of atavism and inherent moral deficiencies. As the popularity of anthropometrical methods declined at the beginning of the twentieth century, psychiatry became the scientific methodology of choice for positivists in the study of criminal behavior. They argued that physical abnormalities were neither necessary nor sufficient to predict criminal tendencies as these stemmed more from the diseases of the mind, rather than those of the body. These studies were rooted in developments in psychiatric discourse of the nineteenth century.

NINETEENTH-CENTURY PSYCHIATRY AND CRIMINAL DANGER IN FRANCE

According to Michel Foucault, a new theory of crime emerged in nineteenth-century France that put forward the conception of a "dangerous individual," whose criminal nature was a social fact *sui generis*, irrespective of actual criminal conduct: "Nineteenth century psychiatry invented an entirely fictitious entity, a crime which is insanity, a crime that is nothing but insanity, an insanity that is nothing but crime" (Foucault 1990, 132). The deviant individual was simultaneously turned into an object of scientific research as well as penal control (Foucault 1979, 191). This concept of a criminal personality became the foundation of the emergent discourses of criminology and penology (Pasquino 1991, 245). The emphasis was as much on knowing and understanding the criminal mind as it was on judging and punishing the crime.

This approach to criminality as a juridical-political process was directly tied to new ways of organizing knowledge. This new penal theory not only was a result of the development of the modern criminal justice apparatuses of the state but also coincided with the discursive and institutional development of psychiatry as a science. The result was the introduction of psychiatrists as experts in the criminal justice system, or what Foucault calls the "psychiatrization of criminal danger" (1990, 128). Thus the psychiatrists of the contemporary era were not only clinical professionals, but they also assumed the added responsibility of fighting against social dangers of crime. The principle of social defense was inherent in the psychiatric and legal discourse on dangerousness. The judgment of crime and punishment was no longer the sole concern of the judicial branches, but also a complex of scientific institutions, practices, and experts.[2] In this era a new criminal subject was born, whose very existence was a danger to the society as she carried within herself the potential of criminal transgression that did not necessarily have to be realized in concrete action. For these individuals, the tenet of "presumption of innocence" which was foundational to classical jurisprudence was suspended, and their guilt was established not by *actus reus*, but by the proclamation of psychiatric professionals. The "scientific-judicial complex" invented the natural criminal who "is responsible since by his very existence he is a creator of risk, even if he is not at fault, since he has not of his free will chosen evil over good" (Foucault 1990, 148).

By the middle of the nineteenth century, a generation of early psychiatrists in France, including Philippe Pinel (1745–1826) and Jean-Étienne Dominique Esquirol (1772–1840), established some of the fundamental precepts and therapies in psychiatry as well as innovative institutional treatment. Pinel was one of the first major figures in French psychiatry, and a significant intellectual inspiration to most other psychologists of the nineteenth century. While Pinel was a physician by profession, his writings show a strong influence of enlightenment philosophy. He saw a clear moral dimension to psychological disorders, and, true to his Enlightenment beliefs, asserted the importance of reclaiming people suffering from mental conditions as healthy and productive members of the society through progressive therapeutic intervention within the asylum framework.

For much of the nineteenth century, not all psychologists made a distinction between physiological and psychological factors, and many identified somatic defects as one of the most important causes of behavioral pathologies. While Pinel did emphasize the importance of diagnosing the somatic conditions especially brain damage caused by organic lesions, he nevertheless recognized pure psychological conditions. His clinical observations diagnosed the existence of psychological maladies in patients who did not show any sign of physiological defects. Thus he asserted that while degenerative conditions of the brain might not be curable, there exist a large number of patients who can be treated as their conditions resulted more from moral rather than somatic defects. Most importantly, he identified a certain condition of mind what he called *manie sans délire*, or "partial insanity," that made the patients susceptible to instinctive fury.

This conception of affective or temporary insanity can be seen as foundational among conceptions of psychopathology and dangerousness as it posited the existence of individuals who do not show any outward signs of insanity or intellectual disabilities and henceforth almost impossible to identify as a threat to public safety. Pinel's protégé Esquirol carried forward on the path established by the former. True to the contemporary traditions of nosology, Esquirol provided an elaborate classification of psychological conditions, and identified *lypemanie* and *monomanie* as the two major forms of insanity. Lypemanie was distinguished by a condition of melancholic disorder, which would be roughly analogous to depression in the current diagnostic frameworks of psychiatry. The term "monomanie," or "monomania," was used to describe a condition marked by obsessive tendencies and paranoia rendering the patients incapable of exercising intellectual or moral judgment.[3] Monomania proved to be a foundational idea in the long history of the conception of dangerousness in legal psychiatry.

Esquirol distinguished between several forms of behavioral deviance stemming from monomaniac conditions including alcoholism, sexual deviance, as well as violent crimes resulting from monomaniac passion including homicide and arson (incendiary monomania) (Esquirol 1845). These result from an uncontrollable destructive urge. People suffering from this condition, according to Esquirol, do not show any sign of insanity at other times until they are consumed with the fury that signals the onset of the condition. Thus the minds of these individuals were cleaved between reason and insanity, and at times there is great struggle between these two until the latter overpowers the former.

> They destroy, in consequence of a blind and momentary disposition, independently of the will. They have an attack of monomania without delirium. Observation demonstrates, that the insane who suffer from homicidal monomania, are, now of a gloomy, melancholic, capricious and passionate disposition; and now, remarkable for the mildness and excellency of their morals and habits. The state of the atmosphere, certain disorders of the organs of nutritive life, over-excitement of the nervous sensibility, vices of education, exaltation of the religious sentiment, the power of imitation, mortifications, and lastly, extreme misery, are the exciting causes of this malady. (Esquirol 1845, 364)

While Pinel and Esquirol established the condition of monomania, it was accorded a new level of importance by Esquirol's student, Etienne-Jean Georget. Georget's work specifically addressed the interface of law and psychiatry especially in the area of criminal procedures. His idea of "homicidal monomania" became a source of some controversy among jurists and medical circles in contemporary France, especially with reference to his commentary on the case of Henriette Cornier, who was accused of a particularly brutal case of child murder in 1825 (Appignanesi 2008). Cornier clearly did not manifest any outward signs of the "madness" and seemed to be perfectly normal in her outward behavior. However, Georget claimed that she is a classic example of a homicidal monomaniac as defined by Esquirol. This case attracted a significant attention not just for the gruesomeness of the crime, but also the intellectual ferment regarding the place of scientific knowledge in the judicial process.

The Cornier case was a milestone in the history of modern legal psychiatry since it established the trend of psychiatric expertise in the judicial process (Foucault 1982, 2004). The *Code Napoleon* did allow for the insanity defense, and psychiatric specialists, including Georget, testified to the fundamental unsoundness of Cornier's mind in spite of the apparent sanity of her behavior. Georget wrote a series of pamphlets commenting on some contemporary murder trials. He argued that only psychiatric specialists can make the correct diagnosis of monomania or other forms of insanity, and decisions of lawyers and judges being devoid of scientific expertise amounted to the miscarriage of justice. This earned Georget a significant amount of public and prosecutorial hostility that had an adverse effect on his later professional career (Goldstein 2002). Regardless of Georget's personal fortune, the salience of psychiatric expertise in criminal trials of our time owes much to him. In the years following the Cornier trial, the idea of monomania came to attain a degree of intellectual cache among educated people beyond psychiatric circles (Goldstein 1991; Van Zuylen 2005).

Early nineteenth-century French psychiatry posited the existence of psychopathological conditions beyond common understanding of insanity that will receive a new lease of life in the twentieth century especially with the rise of Freudianism. It also highlighted the dangers lurking beyond the surface in these individuals—the threat of their uncontrollable fury that could be unleashed on hapless victims when it is triggered by situational conditions. As these individuals constituted a special category of criminals the roots of whose crime were inherent in their psyche that could be deciphered by the specialist knowledge, contemporary psychiatrists also claimed the status of guardians of public safety.

The early nineteenth-century psychiatrists inherited the progressivism of enlightenment and advocated therapeutic rather than penal measures to contain the danger posed by the criminally insane. However, since the middle of the nineteenth century, a new vision of mental disorders related to behavioral deviance emerged in France, and gained currency among many psychiatrists in other nations. The theory of "degeneracy" conceptualized criminality as stemming from organic disorders in the brain and potentially transferred by heredity across generations. Given that the source of the problem was organic lesions in the brain, rather than Pinel's idea of "lesions of reason," proponents of this idea did not see much hope of therapeutic intervention except for incapacitation through indeterminate imprisonment and/or lobotomy. One of the earliest exponents of this theory of psychopathology was Esquirol's student, Jacques-Joseph Moreau (1804–1884).[4] He asserted that insanity as well as genius results from overstimulation of the mind, particularly from the secretion of the organic chemicals in the brain, which causes instability, and eventual decay of the psyche.

Along with Moreau, the other most influential exponent of the theory of degeneracy in contemporary French psychology was Bénédict Augustin Morel (1809–1873). Morel's theory of degeneracy was based on a concept of abnormal evolutionary processes leading to a "morbid deviation" from the natural progress of species. These may be caused by a variety of internal and external conditions, and results in physical and psychological decay in the case of humans, which are evidenced by physical stigmas and behavioral pathologies in these individuals. In elucidating the causes for this degeneracy, Morel presented a whole host of factors including climatic and topographical toxicity believed to be corrosive to the human body and mind. He also believed that these pathologies are hereditary and thereby afflict the stock of the affected individuals for generations until they become extinct from diminishing fertility.

Morel's ideas represented a very powerful discourse in nineteenth-century scientific thought that identified hereditary degeneracy as one of the most serious causes for crime and other social problems. Morel first articulated the core ideas that influenced Lombrosian criminal anthropology and certain forms of eugenic thought that emerged in the early twentieth century. Morel invented a new conception of insanity, or *folie héréditaire,* which included various types of mental disorders arranged according to the seriousness of the condition—people with nervous temperament, alcoholics, morally insane individuals who were inherently dangerous, and people with intellectual disabilities. Morel argued that certain people were more likely to be afflicted by these psychiatric disorders as predispositions to these conditions were transmitted by heredity.

However, his conception of intergenerational inheritance was more complex than most forms of nineteenth-century hereditarianism as he held environmental and genetic conditions equally responsible. People born with conditions such as alcoholism and inebriety created an environment of misery around them affecting their children, who were already genetically predisposed to these vices. He argued that there were certain natural limits to hereditary degeneration as progressive decay of these individuals led to infertility in a few generations. This natural extinction of degeneracy among humans did not safeguard the society from the dangers of the morbid impulses of these individuals and they left a long trail of destruction in their wake.

> The strange and unknown types which people our prisons are not so strange and unknown to those who study the morbid varieties of the human species from the double point of view of the psychic and moral condition of the individuals that compose them. They personify the various degenerations of the species, and the evil which produces them constitutes for modern society a greater danger than the barbaric invasion did for the old. (Morel 1847, quoted in de Quirós 1912, 7)

Morel's work received an enthusiastic endorsement from Theodor Ribot, one of the principal exponents of evolutionary theory in contemporary French psychology (Dowbiggin 1991). Ribot asserted that at the most basic level human consciousness reflects sensations in the nervous system and other organs of the body. Therefore, physiological as well as psychological conditions are subject to the laws of evolution and inheritance (Ribot 1906 [1884]). Most forms of insanity are caused by organic pathologies in the human brain and nervous system, and these morbid organic conditions are hereditary in nature. He argued that in all the cases, hereditary atavism was responsible for the criminal acts and education or environmental factors had little or no influence in taming the instincts that drove individuals to crimes of insanity. Most forms of criminal and deviant behavior stemmed from heritable conditions of the psyche and these instincts and passions became powerful across generations and took the form of a moral insanity over which the offender had little control.

> It were to be wished, in the interest of science, that inquiries should be made as to the progenitors of criminals for at least two or three generations. This would be an excellent means of demonstrating the kinship that exists between those cerebral infirmities which produce the psychic anomalies leading to crime, and the pathological affections of the nerve centers, particularly the brain. The fact, demonstrated by Drs. Ferrus and Lélut, that insanity is much more frequent among criminals than other persons, goes far to prove that crime and insanity are closely connected. The number of criminals whose ancestors have given signs of insanity is very great. (Ribot 1891, 93–94)

A representative of the intellectual culture of imperialism, Ribot's work is quite frank with its prejudices. He added that gypsies and "other inferior races" also showed an innate propensity to go against the morals of civilization, which were inherited along with the desire for vagrancy and rootlessness. He argued that "national character," or the collective psyche of a nation, decided the fates of nations. It was produced by similar laws of physiological and psychological development to those that regulated the character of individuals. The national culture was an expression of the virtues and vices of the people, as the institutions that governed the culture, polity, and the economy of nations were produced by the people of the nation in their own image. Therefore, the underdevelopment of the Asian societies resulted from the superstitions, ignorance, and self-indulgence that reigned supreme in the character of the people and the culture of the nation, leading to moral and physical decay passed across generations (Ribot 1891).

Perhaps the most elaborate contemporary psychological analysis of crime came from Propser Despine, whose magnum opus *Psychologie Naturelle* provided a detailed set of studies of criminal personalities (Despine 1868; Verplaetse 2002). Despine argued that the twin meaning of the word "conscience" in French led to certain semantic confusion among psychologists. He made a distinction between conscience as "moral consciousness" and as "personal consciousness," or the sensory and cognitive faculties of an individual. Like Fournet and Pinel before him, Despine too acknowledged the organic dimension of psychological pathologies (Despine 1875). However, he argued that there were cases of insanity without any corresponding organic pathologies in the brain, where passions or fury overcame moral consciousness as well as cognitive faculties. This might result in criminal derangement beyond the control of the afflicted individuals (Berrios 1996; Despine 1875; Marková 2005). Despine provided an early iteration of the idea of "automatist" theory in psychology (Crabtree 2003). He argued that the inherent psychological instability of these offenders reduced them to mere "automata" whose instincts overpowered their rational or moral sense and thereby they represented a natural danger to the society (Carpentar 1883). Thereby, Despine asserted that normal penal measures were ineffective against these individuals (Despine 1868). Therefore they should rather be incarcerated in "moral hospitals" in the care of alienists who might be able to find a cure for these conditions through scientific investigation of the vagaries of this condition and afflicted individuals (Carlson 2001).

Despine's research was approvingly cited by his contemporaries across the English Channel, Darwin and Galton, in their respective works on the baser instincts of the human mind (Darwin 1871; Galton 1883). Galton made a particularly instructive argument on the dangerous instincts of the criminal who untamed by morality or civilization may wreak havoc on innocent people.

> We must guard ourselves against looking upon vicious instincts as perversions, inasmuch as they may be strictly in accordance with the healthy nature of the man, and, being transmissible by inheritance, may become the normal characteristics of a healthy race, just as the sheep-dog, the retriever, the pointer, and the bull-dog, have their several instincts. . . . The ideal criminal is, unhappily for him, deficient in qualities that are capable of restraining his unkindly or inconvenient instincts; he has neither sympathy for others nor the sense of duty, both of which lie at the base of conscience; nor has he sufficient self-control to accommodate himself to the society in which he has to live, and so to promote his own selfish interests in the long-run. (Galton 1883, 62)

Other contemporary psychiatrists in France, like Fournet, argued that organic and psychological disorders are fundamentally different and thereby should be treated accordingly. Fournet specifically connected morality, reason, and self-awareness in his analysis of psychological disorders, and argued that criminal responsibility should be seen as being proportionate to the degree of self-awareness in the individual (Marková 2005). Another of Esquirol's students, Louis Delasiauve, posited the existence of psychiatric disorders beyond insanity stemming from brain lesions. In his study of epilepsy, he made a distinction between "sympathetic epilepsy," which results from organic pathologies in the brain, and "idiopathic epilepsy," which occurs without any identifiable lesions (Bladin 2001).

The idea of temporary insanity stemming from pathologies of the mind was also was appeared in medical and incipient psychological discourses in the English-speaking world around the same time. This condition was analogous to the theory of "moral insanity" that was a cornerstone of late nineteenth- and early twentieth-century psychiatry in the Anglo-American medical circles (Rafter 2004b). Perhaps the most important work in the genre came from James Cowles Pritchard, a physician from Bristol and a contemporary of Pinel (1786–1848). Pritchard defined moral insanity as a "a morbid perversion of the natural feelings, affections, inclinations, temper, habits, moral dispositions, and natural impulses without any remarkable disorder or defect of the intellect or knowing or reasoning faculties and in particular without any insane delusion or hallucination" (Pritchard 1837, 6). Very much like Pinel and later Esquirol, Pritchard saw this as a new frontier of medical research, as contemporary annals of medicine did not contain any insights on this form of mental disorder beyond the more traditional definitions of total insanity and intelligence deficiencies or "imbecility."

While the idea of "moral insanity" was conceptually similar to Pinel's idea of monomania, both Esquirol and Pritchard sought to distinguish these from one another. In the case of moral insanity, there was no "lesion of understanding," as Esquirol would have it, and Pritchard himself argued that this condition was unique to the extent that there were no other conventional symptoms of mental imbalance such as delusion or fury. While Pritchard initially did not explicitly link moral insanity with somatic conditions of the brain, by the mid-1840s he came to see broad similarities between his work and that of the German psychiatrist Maximilian Jacobi, and posited organic disorders as primary causes for mental pathologies (Augstein 1996). One of the central characteristics of moral insanity for Pritchard was a sense of egocentrism heightened to the extent of obsession and an almost complete disjuncture from fellow members of the community. This way he may seem wedded to a rather old-fashioned sense of morality as community consciousness that was gradually starting to be unraveled by the ideology of individualism in that era of the dawn of industrial modernity. However, twentieth-century psychiatrists would revive the definition of behavioral pathology as lack of concern for others in constructing the idea of sociopathy, or antisocial personality disorder.

Along with Pritchard, Henry Maudsley (1835–1918) was an early exponent of psychopathological theories of insanity. Maudsley held that psychology should be a part of the larger medical discourse, as he saw the study of physiology and pathology of mind being two branches of the same science. He argued that historically the concepts of mind and soul had been conflated to the detriment of science, and the habit of seeing the mind as an intangible or incorporeal entity prevented it from being subject to the same scientific scrutiny as the human body. Psychological pathologies therefore had been rendered incomprehensible by science, and were seen as moral defects and sins that were punished by sending the offender to an asylum, rather than diagnosed and treated as an affliction of the brain and treated as a problem of medicine rather than a crime of weak will or dangerous insanity.

Maudsley also argued that the borderline between sanity and insanity was often hard to define and delineate. This posed simultaneously a medical and a legal difficulty in the diagnosis of insanity and determination of responsibility in criminal cases. The legal definition of madness was often completely devoid of any scientific understanding of the diseases of the mind, much less that the individuals' motives were beyond comprehension for sane people. People suffering from mental conditions were seldom completely incapable of reason—they often had psychological profiles and emotions very similar to those of sane individuals. The crucial difference was that the former were often incapable of exercising the restraints on their emotions that is the hallmark of sanity. This posed a problem for jurisprudence and penology, as a person who suffered from an inherent defect of reason and moral restraint was really not the same as an offender who was fully aware of the consequences of her or his action. At the same time, there had to be penal consequences for offenders suffering from psychological disorders, since not doing so would create a moral hazard for the entire society. Therefore, the need of the day was a scientific intervention rather than a simple penal one, and the right place for a deranged offender was the asylum and not a prison cell.

Echoing the scientific gestalt of contemporary positivism, Maudsley argued that human volition or will was not a metaphysical entity. Rather, it was dependent on the processes of the brain and the nervous system (1874). Thereby disorders in the motor centers of the nervous system led to mental derangement and the loss of rational faculties and moral senses in the affected individual. Mental processes—including emotions, thoughts, and rational faculties—were controlled or affected by the organic processes in the body, and consequently anatomy was indeed destiny, as free will in humans was circumscribed by physiology.[5] Maudsley made a conceptual distinction between moral insanity of monomania and the moral imbecility that stemmed from hereditary factors. The latter was a distinct class of criminals characterized by low physical and mental characteristics and whose lives were marked by intemperance or debauchery. This class spawned generations of degenerate beings and their physiognomy was marked by the stigma of their heredity: "They are scrofulous, not seldom deformed, with badly-formed angular heads; are stupid, sullen, sluggish, deficient in vital energy, and sometimes afflicted with epilepsy. As a class, they are of mean and deficient intellect, though excessively cunning, and not a few of them are weak-minded and imbecile" (1874, 30). The idea of hereditary defects, sometimes manifested in somatic abnormalities that Lombroso also claimed to be the most important source of criminal danger, was a recurring theme in nineteenth-century medicine and psychiatry. It found the fullest expression in the eugenic discourse that was established by Francis Galton in the United Kingdom.

THE ORIGIN OF EUGENICS: HEREDITY, VIRTUE, AND CONTROLLING REPRODUCTION

Galton, a Victorian era scientist and cousin of Darwin, coined the term *eugenics*, literally meaning "well born" in ancient Greek. A renaissance figure, Galton was a towering personality in contemporary Anglo-American scientific circles, and made pioneering contributions to the developing sciences of anthropology, biology, meteorology, psychology, and statistics. Influenced by Darwin's theory of evolution, especially the theory of natural selection, his main area of inquiry was the intergenerational transmission of genetic characteristics. In a two-part article published in 1865 in *Macmillan's Magazine*, Galton provided a preliminary sketch of a theory that would influence an array of figures as disparate as Woodrow Wilson and Adolf Hitler over the next sixty years.

Galton's theory of eugenics was based on the observation that a relatively small number of British families have produced a disproportionately large number of important figures in almost all fields of social life. He asserted that intelligence and other necessary qualities for success found among these families result from their hereditary biological nature, rather than advantages that may come with wealth and social positions. Galton's initial formulation of the theory was based on a very limited sample of six contemporary eminent figures and their illustrious relatives. However, Galton provided a more elaborate account of eugenics over the next forty years. In a more elaborate formulation of his theory of heredity published in a book titled *Hereditary Genius* (1870), Galton made a chart of natural abilities among people in contemporary Britain with seven grades of on each side of the median. He claimed that out of every one million people there are about two hundred fifty "eminent" people—that is, people who are five grades above the median of natural abilities and who are at the vanguard of their professions. In a manner much similar to Friedrich Nietzsche and other thinkers who exalted the role of *übermensch* and saw democracy as glorifying the lowest common denominators of the society, Galton was not particularly appreciative of the masses. Indeed, he argued that celibacy and late marriages among university men result in the relative decrease in the people of superior morality and abilities that may result in a decline of civilization of the West.

In the late 1870s Galton became involved in building a model of statistical probability for predicting hereditary transmission of qualities. He supervised a large-scale anthropometric study undertaken during the International Health Exhibition in London in 1884, in which more than nine thousand people were measured for height, weight, reflexes, and varieties of sensory perception. Based on his calculation of the probabilities of genetic inheritance, Galton established some of the first laws of statistical inference of correlation and regression that would be perfected by his protégé Karl Pearson (Galton 1889). For Galton, the practical implications of his calculations were quite clear. In arguing that talents as well as vices are products of heredity to a very large extent, Galton established what he saw as a manifesto for the betterment of the human race through controlling reproduction. He argued that the "inborn quality" or "stock" of its population is one of the most important resources in any society. Therefore, the improvement of "health, energy, ability, manliness and courteous disposition" that marks the best among any population will result in all-around betterment of the society. This, according to him, is the ultimate goal of eugenics, that of ultimate benefit and welfare of the mankind through scientific intervention in the lives of the people. In a speech to the *Sociological Society of London* he outlined some of the fundamental precepts of eugenics—a clarion call to the scientific community to join this revolutionary doctrine (Galton 1905).

A foremost objective for eugenicists was the scientific task of methodical study and dissemination of information regarding the laws of heredity. This also included an inquiry into the historical evolution of talent, enterprise, and other desirable qualities among a select group of families in a nation. This needs to be complemented by studies of the civic usefulness of the various classes with their rate of reproduction. Decline of the number of upper classes and the increase in the number of the undesirables would lead to a degeneration and eventual decline of the fortune of the entire nation. He argued that one of the most efficient ways of achieving the goal of "race-betterment" would be the regulation of population by encouraging the reproduction of the fittest, and discouraging the reproduction of the unfit, the deficient, and the dangerous. He argued that the charitable treatment of habitual criminals and the feebleminded only leads to the continuation of their depredations, and overpopulation of "low-class offsprings." Therefore governmental aid and opportunity of education to these groups need to be limited or eliminated for the welfare of the entire society. He also urged the competent authorities to establish a system of issuing certificates to people regarding their eugenic fitness (Galton 1905, 23). Ultimately, eugenics needed to be embraced by the nation as a new religion and assimilated in its conscience (Galton 1904). Remarking on the tremendous influence of religion in social relations, Galton declared that science ought to be elevated to a similar position in modern societies. Therefore, the superstitions and taboos that have governed the relations between people would be replaced with the rational laws of scientific certainty. Eugenics for Galton represented a "far sighted philanthropy" and a "higher conception of patriotism" (Galton 1905). Most importantly, eugenics stood for the best hopes of modern science, that of improving the conditions of the human race by manipulating the forces of nature.

While Galton established the principles of eugenics, his work was not directly concerned with the question of crime though it was broadly concerned with the long term threats to the welfare of the British society based on his assessment of demographic trends. For Galton and his followers, the clear and present danger stemmed from the discrepancy in the birth rate between the upper and the working classes. Galton's protégé Karl Pearson forcefully argued that the long-term prosperity of the British society was at risk due to the high rate of birth among the working classes and consequent weakening of the national stock (Pearson 1901).

Scholars have argued that eugenics emerged as an ideology of the professional middle class in its attempt to establish its position as the harbingers of scientific modernity, and clearly mark its social distinction from the traditional aristocracy and the teeming working masses in England. The eugenic movement in Britain achieved very moderate success. A laboratory for eugenic studies was established in University of London, and the British eugenicists also formed the Eugenics Education Society. However, the eugenicists in Britain did not manage to effect far-reaching legislative measures. The only instance of eugenic legislation, the Mental Deficiency Act of 1913, did not authorize segregation, incarceration, or sterilization of individuals diagnosed with any intellectual disability (Kevles 1985). However, eugenics managed to find a very receptive audience further west, across the Atlantic Ocean. In the United States, the appeal of eugenics was not just limited to scientists and other members of the professional middle classes, but also in political and governmental circles. There emerged a new conception of criminal danger, and some of the first eugenic laws aimed at preventing the reproduction of the unfit, the criminal, and the "defective delinquents" were passed in the United States.

NOTES

1. Quetelet famously called his craft "social physics," thereby depriving August Comte of his first choice for the name of a new science that would later be called sociology.
2. This coincided with the nineteenth-century concern of "individualization" in the criminal justice system.
3. Esquirol was also an important figure in the institutional development of psychiatry. He conducted extensive research on mental institutions across Europe, and headed the *Charenton* asylum in Paris. Many of his recommendations on the organization and practical matters in asylums were incorporated in the 1838 mental health law in France.
4. He was also known as for his extensive travels in Asia. Moreau is famous in the annals of modern medicine and psychiatry for his pioneering experiments in and writings on the effects of psychotropic and hallucinogenic narcotic substances.
5. Maudsley provided scientific excuses for legitimizing patriarchy by delineating a natural basis of male dominance. He argued that gender differences are not products of morality, customs, or laws of a society—it is a plain biological fact determined by reproductive organs, and only mutilation or natural dysfunctions of the body could bring about equality among men and women! "While woman preserves her sex, she

will necessarily be feebler than man, and, having her specific bodily and mental characters, will have to a certain extent her own sphere of activity; where she has become thoroughly masculine in nature, or hermaphrodite in mind—when, in fact, she has pretty well divested herself of her sex—then she may take his ground, and do his work; but she will have lost her feminine attractions, and probably also her chief feminine functions" (1872, 35).

TWO

Eugenics and Hereditarianism in the United States

The eugenic movement in the United States rose to prominence at the end of the nineteenth century. At the end of the Gilded Age and the beginning of the Progressive era, the combined forces of industrialization, urbanization, and immigration were radically transforming the nation. The reform agenda of the progressive era therefore revolved around the concern for mitigating the potentially destructive effects of industrialism and the erosion of the traditional values by an ambitious program of social regulation and control. Many contemporary reformers and intellectuals saw the principal utility of the natural sciences as being the ability to analyze, understand, and ultimately control the forces of nature. Similarly, they envisioned the true telos of the social and behavioral sciences as assuming the same role in the social world by facilitating the rational understanding, prediction, and control of human action. Scientific expertise was not seen as an end in itself, but rather as a means to rationally order the society by controlling the more disruptive or destructive forces inherent in human nature.

A generation of scholars, social workers, and philanthropists advocated the need for a social technology, akin to those in the natural sciences, that would effectively diagnose and possibly cure the ills of the society. Therefore, the human sciences including psychology, sociology, jurisprudence, and penology, took on a new importance in the eyes of contemporary reformers, scholars, philanthropists, and administrators for their utility in understanding and predicting human action, and consequently in rationalizing the modes of social control. Inspired by the emergent perspective of positivism, many contemporary social scientists believed in the need for social control through the application of scientific theories (Ross 1901). John Dewey asserted that advances in the physical sciences have led to the greater degree of control and consequent taming of the vagaries of nature as well as increase in material wellbeing. Thus psychology and the social sciences need to follow the same path at the mental and social realms of human life, which would result in the same degree of control in the "ethical sphere" (Dewey 1900, 124).

The role of the social sciences in aiding agents and institutions of social control should be seen in its historical context (Ross 1984). For the Progressive-era scholars and reformers, the idea of social control was not necessarily seen in an authoritarian or elitist sense. It implied normative integration of society through scientific understanding and regulation of human behavior. The scientific analysis and understanding of human behavior was simply a way of minimizing threats to collective well-being that came from the indeterminacy of human thought and action and the danger of widespread moral transgression and breakdown of social norms brought forth by the rapidity of economic and technological change.

EUGENICS AND DEFECTIVE DELINQUENCY

The Progressive-era faith in rational governance led to a greater appreciation of the need of scientific understanding of social problems. Thus a key strategy adopted by many of the reformers took the form of surveys, research reports, and other forms of studies that addressed the issue of crime in society. Many of the contemporary studies of criminality posited the importance of understanding hereditary traits of delinquency. Robert Dugdale, in a study titled *The Jukes* (1876), provided one of the earliest accounts of hereditary criminality. Dugdale's study begun in 1874 when he made a fact-finding tour of thirteen county jails at the behest of the New York Prison Association. By his account, he found an interesting similarity between the cases of six different inmates with different family names. Upon further inquiry, he established that they were all blood relatives in a lineage that stretched back to the early colonial era. Dugdale argued that his calculations show a positive link between heredity and behavior. However, he pointed out that statistical studies of heredity could only indicate the probability of inheritance of pathological traits across generations. They cannot predict with certainty the fate of each individual, and it is important to synthesize statistics with "historico-biographical" analysis of individuals to elicit a more accurate analysis of their lives and action (Dugdale 1910 [1876], 12).

He studied the effects of consanguineous and marriage relations in the long lineage of the Jukes, and found that the entire lineage divided into branches with distinctive hereditary qualities, including positive ones such as industriousness, and negative ones such as criminality, pauperism, and sexual licentiousness. He found that pauperism was inherited across consanguineous lines, and criminal tendencies were carried through illegitimate male progenies of the members of the greater Juke clan through their legitimate and illegitimate unions. Similarly, he identified a prevalence of "harlotry," or licentiousness, among the female members of the clan. Dugdale claimed that a primary cause for delinquent behavior was the presence of constitutional pathologies among the members of the clan. At the same time, Dugdale's study did not show the kind of genetic determinism present in much of later eugenic thought. Indeed, he argued that environmental factors mediated and mitigated the effect of genetic inheritance of the individual, and many of the members of the Juke clan escaped the infamy of the bloodline by growing up in more salubrious surroundings (Dugdale 1910 [1876], 113).

While Dugdale established the basis of hereditarian theories of the subsequent generations, he did not present a cohesive theory of heritable delinquency or criminal danger as the science of genetics was yet to emerge in his time. His explanation of the Juke clan was to a very large extent inductive, and it did not really provide a basis for generalization. He claimed that his own research on a sample of the prison population in the New York State penitentiary system pointed to the presence of hereditary pathologies among many criminals especially among habitual offenders. But he conceded that a more systematic inquiry of the topic was hindered by the lack of statistical data on crime in the country. He argued that a large number of prisoners were of sound mind and health and had committed offenses due to situational factors. However, there was also a correspondingly large proportion of prisoners whose criminal tendencies were rooted in a diseased body or psyche, and this group could not be reformed through regular penal sentences and the probation and parole system. They had to be permanently incapacitated by indeterminate sentences in order prevent them from bringing to the world their "noisome progeny" that might result in the "extinction of their race" (Dugdale 1910, 114). Dugdale argued that a scientific perspective on crime should be modeled on medicine in the latter's pursuit of causes, conditions, symptoms, and ultimately the curing of morbid conditions in order to cure this disease of the body social.

Dugdale's study spawned a whole host of family studies (Rafter 1988).[1] Perhaps the most influential text in this genre was Henry Goddard's *The Kallikak Family*. This book was a first in a series of work Goddard published through the 1910s and early 1920s that became some of the foundational texts in eugenics. Goddard worked as the director of the psychological research laboratory at the Training School for Feebleminded Boys and Girls in Vineland, New Jersey, in the early 1900s. The book was based on the genealogy of a student called Deborah Kallikak (Goddard 1912).[2] The family tree was traced to a soldier during the Civil War who sired two different families: one based on his union with a "feebleminded" woman, and the other based on his marriage with a "well-born" woman. Goddard provided elaborate diagrams of the family tree that showed a clear division between normalcy and pathology in the two branches of the family.

While hereditarian thought, as well as the connection between feeblemindedness and delinquent behavior, was coming into prominence at that time, there was little consensus regarding the methodology of establishing intellectual or cognitive disabilities. Psychologists in Europe and the United States had been concerned with the issue of categorizing and classifying levels of intelligence and cognitive abilities since the late nineteenth century (Cattell 1890; Ireland 1877; Trent 1995; Wilbur 1877). However, none of these efforts were widely accepted as comprehensive scales of intelligence (Zenderland 1998). Thus Goddard sought to forge a new direction in psychometric research that would establish an objective basis of determining the influence of heredity on human behavior based on emergent discourses of intelligence testing in educational psychology and Mendelian genetics in evolutionary biology.

A complete analysis of Mendelian genetics is beyond the scope of this work, but a brief summary of his principal discovery is warranted, as it would illustrate the ways in which it was adopted by eugenic biologists. Gregor Mendel's experimentation with pea plants showed that certain characters of hybrid varieties very closely resemble those of the parent plants, whereas certain characters are less visible, or what he called "segregated" between "dominant" and "recessive" characters across generations. These "unit characters" are inherent in the "germ plasms" of the plants, and during the process of fertilization *similar allelomorphs* produce *homozygotes* that bear these dominant characteristics, and *dissimilar allelomorphs* produce *heterozygotes*, which bear characters created by the combination of these allelomorphs, and the recessive characters are carried across generations in an infinity of permutations and combinations.

One of the foremost exponents of evolutionary biology among the eugenicists was Charles Davenport—a biologist who founded the Eugenics Records Office in Cold Spring Harbor Laboratory in Nassau County, New York. In Davenport's view, Mendel's observations regarding pea plants also held true for human heredity. Humans inherit physical characteristics from their parents and ancestors in very much the same way; they also inherit a complex totality of mental and sensory traits as well. In the union between two people, if one carries a certain strain and the other does not, then their offspring inherit this strain in a diluted form as a *heterozygous* factor. However, when both the parents have a certain characteristic this trait is carried forward across generations through multiple permutations and combinations.

> Where two such individuals possessing a heterozygous character marry each other, then, on the average, one-fourth of the offspring will result from the union of two germ cells possessing the character, two-fourths from one

> germ cell possessing and one lacking the character, and one-fourth from two germ cells lacking the character—children from two such germ cells will, of course, be without the character even though both of their parents possess it. (Davenport 1909, 18)

Davenport claimed that much of contemporary jurisprudence was based on the mistaken assumption that all individuals are free agents who are capable of rational thought. He argued that a high frequency of delinquency among certain family lines as evidenced by Dugdale's study of the Jukes, as well as other family studies, provides ample evidence that strains of delinquency are carried across generations through heredity. He listed a long set of characteristics—including "lydactylism," "syndactylism," "haemophilia," "night blindness," "congenital cataract," "color blindness," "keratosis palmoe," and "albinism"—that are inherited by the Mendelian principles. At the same time, he took quite a leap of faith in arguing that along with physiological characteristics, intellectual and moral capacities are transmitted in the very same way. Thus, the progeny of two defective people will inherit the same defects and carry on with the same kind of life as environment or education play scant role in taming our instincts (1909, 19). He carries this genetic (or germ-plasmic) determinism to its logical conclusion in suggesting that genius, idiocy, and everything in between are products of traits inherent in the germplasma without distinguishing between physiological and behavioral traits. Davenport offered a relatively weak explanation of genetic transmission of traits by suggesting that hormonal secretions from endocrine glands simultaneously determine physical and psychological characteristics. The "quantity and quality" of hormones are determined by the idiosyncrasies of the enzymes of the germ cells (Davenport 1921, 395).

EUGENICS AND INTELLIGENCE TESTING IN THE UNITED STATES

Initially, Goddard continued with the methodology established by nineteenth-century psychologists following Galton's pioneering work in administering psychophysical tests such as physical response time to commands, as well as anthropometric measurements (Zenderland 1998). However, the tests did not provide valid and reliable measurements of intelligence, and Goddard found a new inspiration in the works of Alfred Binet, a French psychologist who recently developed a test for measuring the mental aptitude of school children. Goddard and other American eugenicists adopted and modified these tests as a scientific methodology of measuring intelligence, and hence the capacity of moral reasoning and criminal danger.

A study of Binet's own writing, however, shows that his goals were much more modest and he never viewed his tests to be the only definitive measure of intelligence, nor did he ever claimed to have built a theory of intellectual aptitude based on these measurements (Gould 1981). His aim was simply to provide a practical tool of measuring and grading the cognitive perception of school children. In designing an objective measure of intelligence, Binet worked under the guiding assumption that cognitive abilities can be measured by a scale that would grade and classify people according to their mental age or intellectual maturity. The scale was based on the scores of a series of tests designed to measure multiple dimensions of cognitive abilities, including memory, visual perception, comprehension, analytical abilities, time perception, and so on.

The success of Binet's research was partly due to the fact that he broke with the methods pioneered by Galton and championed by contemporary psychologists, and focused on measuring logical capabilities as the key to understanding intelligence rather than sensorimotor skills or anthropometric measurements (Binet and Simon 1905; Gould 1981). This decoupling of intelligence from physical deformities, cranial features, or microcephalia would prove to be a bridge to twentieth-century psychology and the gradual decline of phrenology and anthropometrical perspectives in the understanding of the human mind in general and intelligence or cognition in particular.

The first scale was introduced in 1905, and comprised of thirty tests arranged in increasing order of complexity (Binet and Simon 1905). The scale of 1905 was primarily designed to identify children with marked mental deficiencies, but it was limited to the extent that it could not grade children according to their apparent mental age (Coxe 1916). Binet and Simon introduced a new scale in 1908, which had an enhanced array of tests, and was specifically designed to measure intelligence, perception, and logical abilities with reference to a normal level for that specific age group. Every subject was given a test designed for a certain age group, and the successful answering of all but one of the tests proved that the subjects' cognitive capacities were average and above for that age group. The subject was given one extra year of additional credit for successful completion of every five tests above this level, and the tests extended up to thirteen years of age. The final version of the Binet-Simon scale that was published in 1911 had five standard tests for each group, and extended the tests to the age of fifteen years, though tests were not administered to children aged eleven, thirteen, and fourteen years (Binet 1911a; Kuhlman 1918).

Perhaps the most important characteristic of the Binet-Simon scale was measuring intelligence with reference to age standards, which allowed for aggregation and standardization of age-graded levels of intelligence. It also facilitated the measurement of cognitive aptitudes of individuals with reference to their age-peers, thereby being able to discern superior or inferior cognitive aptitudes with reference to the age average. At the same time, it also established a new way of defining mental aptitudes in general and intelligence in particular. Binet did not see intelligence as an innate, structural property of the mind; he rather saw it as a dynamic process that involves the use of mental faculties such as memory, attention, and imagination in order to rationally think and decide on a certain course of action. Thus intelligence involved deciding on an objective to be attained, calculate the different paths of achieving it, and, finally, choosing a certain direction judged as the correct one under the circumstances (Binet and Simon 1909; Terman 1916a). Binet also assumed maturity as a primary variable when it comes to these abilities, and therefore the tests were organized according to mental age-specific questions/problems with an increasing level of difficulty.

The Binet-Simon scale provided the basic framework of analysis for American psychologists, though many of them modified and extended the operational details of the tests (Goddard 1911; Huey 1908; Kuhlmann 1918; Pyle 1912; Terman 1916a; Wallin 1913; Yerkes 1916). Lewis Terman, a psychologist at Stanford University, introduced the so-called Stanford Revision of the Binet-Simon scale in 1916 (Terman 1916a). In spite of his admiration for Binet's pioneering work, Terman found what he saw as serious flaws in the methodology that were barriers to the application of the general population. As these were primarily designed for school children, these did not focus so much on adults and therefore the tests required revision in order to measure more mature intelligence levels (Terman 1916a, 51). The Stanford Revision comprised six standardized tests for each age group between the ages three and eighteen, adding several criteria for measuring various forms of mental aptitude that augmented the tests administered by the Binet system. However, unlike the latter, it was specifically designed to be able to be administered to an adult population. While the Binet system established the fundamentals of intelligence testing, it was Terman who popularized the idea of "intelligence quotient," coined by William Stern, and the infamous bell-shaped curve of distribution of intelligence within a group (1916a, 55).

Terman, with his association with the eugenic movement and some racial observations, has earned a degree of notoriety. However, it must be noted that he was rather circumspect about the generalizability of the test data, and argued for complementing these with other scientific procedures (1916a, 1916b). Terman made a distinction between the intellectual and social dimensions of feeblemindedness. In his opinion, intellectual disability could be diagnosed by intelligence tests, but it did not necessarily translate into behavioral or social pathologies, which were influenced by social, economic, and environmental factors (Terman 1916b).

At the same time he added that there appears to be an overwhelming amount of evidence suggesting a strong link between feeblemindedness and delinquency as evidenced by contemporary research. Terman, very much like Goddard and many other psychologists of the time, assumed feeblemindedness to be the most prominent psychological cause for criminal or deviant behavior. The nineteenth-century monographs on the prevalence of delinquency among certain families did identify a high frequency of behavioral pathologies. But these could only identify the more extreme forms of feeblemindedness as they lacked the scientific methods to identify more advanced cases of intellectual disabilities.

Terman asserted that positivist criminologists following Lombroso had erred in emphasizing physiological deformities without understanding the true importance of psychological deficiency as a causative factor for criminal behavior. In many cases, the stigmas identified by Lombroso and his followers were nothing but physical manifestation of psychological pathologies (1916a, 7). As Lombroso drew a direct link between physical stigmas, evolutionary atavism, and criminal behavior, Terman also saw intellectual deficiency as the prime cause of quasi-atavistic lack of moral consciousness, or what he saw as a prerequisite for wayward sensibilities. A mature sense of morality comes only from normal intellectual development, and thus human instincts uninhibited by moral scruples and requisite intelligence are very likely to commit delinquent acts (1916a, 12). Terman, however, conceded that psychological factors such as fear, anxiety, docility, suggestibility, emotional volatility, and other volitional and moral qualities played a role in the determination of "social fitness" (1916b, 533). He argued that quantitative estimation of intelligence did not rule out other nonintellectual factors, and indeed these might be connected in complex ways in determining the behavioral traits of an individual.

The 1910s generated a significant amount of intellectual ferment on the topic of intelligence testing well beyond the walls of academia. At the same time, there was also a lack of consensus about the correct methodology among scholars and practitioners alike. While the Binet-Simon tests and the Stanford Revision determined intelligence quotients based on a correlation between mental and chronological age, a competing system established by Robert M. Yerkes proposed the need for a linear scale independent of the age of subjects. Yerkes, a psychologist working at Harvard University and Boston Psychopathic Hospital, was particularly interested in primate behavior. He underlined the basic similarities in the cognitive processes of humans and apes, and argued that the study of primates might provide clues to human behavior, as the basic behavioral mechanisms were not obscured by cultural influences in the latter (Yerkes 1943, 3).

Yerkes acknowledged Binet's pioneering contribution to the field and adopted many of the same questions/problems. Nevertheless, he argued that scores ranged in a single, universal continuum allowed for better measuring intelligence for purposes of aggregation and comparison rather than a series of discrete age groups. The point-scale method also claimed an advance by expanding the focus to include a wider range of mental functions in order to elicit a more holistic view of intellectual faculties of an individual. Yerkes and his colleagues sought to examine four major groups of cognitive processes: receptivity, including sensibility, perceptivity, discrimination, and association; constructive imagination and memory; affectivity, including feeling, emotions, volition, and suggestibility; and thought, including ideation, judgment, and reasoning (Yerkes, Bridges, and Hardwick 1915, 166–67). Each of these categories was worth fifty points, with a grand total of two hundred points. In order to determine a person's intelligence, her or his score was compared to the average score of her or his peers in a certain class. In order to place an individual within a certain class, Yerkes and his colleagues considered a wide range of sociological variables, such as age, gender, socioeconomic status, primary language, race, and ethnic identity.

Though the point scale and the Binet methods were rival methods, Yerkes collaborated with some of the principal proponents of the latter, including Goddard and Terman, in designing a series of intelligence tests administered on military personnel under the auspices of the Department of Defense. These comprised three separate tests: Alpha tests were administered to service people with some amount of formal education, and those who failed it were administered the Beta test, which mostly involved visual perception tests. The last one involved individualized examination of a select group who failed the Beta test in order to measure the magnitude of their cognitive disabilities. While these tests were extensively used by the Department of Defense subsequently, latter-day scholars have pointed out that the way these were designed put new immigrants at a disadvantage as these were composed of language, history, and general knowledge tests which were much more familiar to native-born Americans (Gould 1981).

Like Terman, Yerkes argued that intelligence scores should be one among many factors considered by the criminal justice system in ascertaining the true causes for delinquency. Thus criminologists should consider family history and circumstances of heredity, environmental factors, physical and medical history, sociability, and other mental traits demonstrated in vocational relations, as well as a thorough psychological examination, to ascertain mental conditions in order to assess the nature of the individual in question. However, certain mental and cognitive conditions such as motor abilities, sensory and receptive functions, perceptual characteristics, attention, memory, imagination, ideation, associative tendencies, reasoning, volitional control, suggestibility, instincts, affectivity, emotions, and moral consciousness should be of a special interest, as these are particularly important in the determination of behavioral pathologies (Yerkes 1916).

The discourse on the scientific diagnosis and legal necessity of regulating the so-called feebleminded came a full circle in the writings of Harry Laughlin, a protégé and colleague of Davenport in the Eugenics Records Office. Laughlin provided a lengthy analysis of the various modes of diagnosis of hereditary degeneracy and delinquency from a eugenic point of view. He argued that unlike mathematics or engineering, the methodology of eugenic diagnosis is not exact since there are too many factors involved in the processes of heredity. However, he held that application of scientific principles along with prudence and experience might yield more reliable diagnoses of the risk factors. The principles of diagnosis of degeneracy included establishing the "pedigree facts," or a comprehensive inventory of genealogy that allowed for a precise tracing of descent and hereditary traits transmitted across generations and different branches of the family tree. Laughlin lauded the work of the eugenic field workers who began with a single subject, or a *propositus*, and collected elaborate data on their family history. Their inquiries put a special emphasis on repeated cases of delinquency within the extended family line. However, he conceded that the work of producing pedigree facts was limited by the availability of records, and while in most cases interviews with friends, neighbors, and acquaintances provided the necessary information, there were still a number of cases where adequate information was not available. The pedigree facts needed to be combined with an inventory of hereditary traits that had been "established" by expert eugenic scientists (Laughlin 1922).

At the same time, Laughlin acknowledged some of the practical problems associated with making a eugenic diagnosis. Other than a small number of homozygotes, the hereditary traits carried forth in the germ plasm became difficult to establish, given the long history of interbreeding across generations for most individuals. Laughlin identified three types of single unit traits—that is, traits that are borne by a single germ plasm. Recessive traits disappear in the first generation if both the parents are not carrying it, though these may resurface later by skipping a few generations. Dominant traits of a parent individual are those that prevail upon the traits of the other parent if he or she is not carrying it, and they are very much visible in the offspring without skipping a generation. There are also a series of traits that are sex-specific, dominant in males and recessive in females—for instance, color blindness and hemophilia. In a union between a man possessing the trait and an unaffected women, the male offspring will be unaffected but half the female offspring will be likely to carry it as a recessive trait, which may be passed on to successive generations (Laughlin 1922, 365).

Laughlin also created an elaborate typology of the so-called socially inadequate category including ten main categories of "feebleminded," "insane," "criminalistic," "epileptic," "inebriate," "diseased," "blind," "deaf," "deformed," and "dependent"—that is, "ne'er-do-wells," "paupers" and "tramps." Laughlin called for a closer integration between law and science in determining the threshold of normalcy, with the eugenicist acting as the scientific expert who will provide the testimony on which the court should base its decision on individual cases. Perhaps Laughlin's greatest contribution to the eugenic discourse was his attempt to formulate legislations based on scientific principles for controlling the social danger of the "socially inadequate" (Laughlin 1922).

There were two intertwined axes of the eugenic discourse to conceptualize dangerousness—on one hand, the measurement of intelligence to determine moral capacity (by the psychologists like Goddard, Terman, or Yerkes), and the hereditary transmission thereof (biologists influenced by Mendelian genetics like Davenport or Laughlin). Both these came together in the defective delinquency laws passed in the United States in the 1910s.

EUGENICS AND LAW

There was a general consensus among eugenicists on the principal of social protection from the dangers inherent in the feebleminded population. This danger, however, had nothing directly to do with actual behavioral patterns or actions of specific individuals all the time. Feeblemindedness was created as a psychosocial category, where the alleged psychological reality of low intelligence not only made the individual less than a perfect citizen, but also guilty of the possibility of causing harm to the normal citizens irrespective of his or her actions in reality. Goddard argued that as the "feebleminded" are not capable of exercising moral judgment and "free will," they should not be treated as common criminals. Rather, with a proper system of psychiatric surveillance, they could be identified and institutionalized before they commit a crime and thereby the society would be safe from the inherent danger of delinquency stemming from mental deficiency (Goddard 1915).

Very much like crime, immigration was another fiercely debated issue of the time. Some invoked the specter of "race suicide" that might result from unchecked influx of allegedly "inferior" people from Europe in arguing for imposing severe restrictions on immigration. Goddard was invited to Ellis Island to study newly arriving immigrants and to administer Binet-Simon tests in 1913. He reported that an overwhelming proportion of immigrants from southern and eastern Europe were found to be feebleminded (Goddard 1917). Scientists also played a direct and official role on the debate on undesirable aliens of the era. Laughlin was appointed as an expert eugenical agent of the U.S. House Committee on Immigration and Naturalization in 1920. By testifying that immigrants from southern and eastern Europe were disproportionately represented in the U.S. penitentiaries and mental institutions, Laughlin argued this would lead to a decline of the racial purity of the nation (Laughlin 1923). Scholars have commented that eugenic advocacy of contemporary scientists played a significant role in shaping public opinion against immigration that ultimately led to the passage of the Immigration Restriction Act

(1921) and Immigration Act of 1924 that established the quota system to limit immigration of the "undesirable" races (Gould 1981; Kevles 1985; Smith 1985).

The contemporary eugenicists advocated for more enduring measures to stop the spread of feeblemindedness within the country. Judge Harry Olson of the Illinois Supreme Court, a key figure in the eugenic movement and the founder of the Psychopathic Laboratory in Chicago, advocated compulsory sterilization, which he (along with many other scientists, jurists, and lay persons) saw as an enduring solution to the menace of feeblemindedness (Olson 1925; Willrich 1998, 2003). The legal assumptions underlying the defective delinquency laws were based on a eugenic reading of the biological sciences and medicine, rather than the political ideals of democracy or classical Enlightenment jurisprudence.

In the case of defective delinquents, the psychological deficiency of intellect established through standardized tests and eugenic examinations was regarded as the source of the incapacity of exercising moral judgment that forms the basis of establishment of guilt or innocence for "normal" defendants. Some opined that defective delinquent could not plead the insanity defense since their cases were not a product of temporary insanity or treatable mental disorders, but a whole lifetime of inherent moral defects stemming from subnormal mental capacities. Henry Ballantine, the dean of the College of Law of University of Illinois, argued that while feebleminded people could not be seen as common criminals, as they were incapable of exercising moral judgment, it was all the more necessary to apprehend, judge, and segregate them for collective security (Ballantine 1919).

By evoking the social defense principle, contemporary eugenicist legal professionals emphasized the preemption of the possibility of crime or the danger that is inherent in all feebleminded people, as normal principle of rehabilitation of criminals did not apply to them. This put the psychiatrists and other scientists of the eugenic persuasion at odds with the legal framework of the Enlightenment in general, and the U.S. Constitution in particular. The eugenicists railed against the "unscientific" basis of law in its insistence of judging concrete behavior, and the perception of equality of all citizens in its eyes. Their rallying cry was the suspension of these "archaic" legal principles and the legislation of new laws based on science, rather than morality or politics, that would forward the cause of social defense.

Perhaps the most infamous legacy of the eugenic movement in the United States was the involuntary sterilization statutes passed in the first two decades of the twentieth century (Black 2004). Proponents of compulsory sterilization of the feebleminded won their first legislative success in Indiana in 1907.[3] The Indiana statute authorized chief administrators of prisons to appoint a committee of medical and psychological experts to examine every inmate for congenital and hereditary mental disabilities. If so diagnosed, the prison authorities were authorized to carry out surgical sterilization procedures so that these conditions were not transmitted to others (Hunter 1914).

The Indiana statute provided the model for sterilization laws in other states. Within two years, three more states—California, Connecticut, and Washington—passed similar bills. In all these cases, the professional committee has a wide discretionary power in deciding the necessity of sterilization. California authorized the resident physicians in the penitentiaries to sterilize any recidivist convicted of violent or sexual crimes in the prison who did not show any indication of moral improvement (Reilly 1991, 48). In 1922, Laughlin drafted a model bill for eugenic sterilization that advocated compulsory sterilization for the "socially inadequate," including the feebleminded, the insane, criminals, epileptics, alcoholics, blind persons, deaf persons, deformed persons, and indigent persons (Laughlin 1922). By that time legislatures of thirty states had passed sterilization of bills.[4]

In certain states the primary purpose of sterilization was punitive as well as preventive and people accused of certain sexual offenses were surgically castrated. This was relatively rare, and found only in the statute books of California, Washington, and North and South Dakota. In most of these cases, the statutes applied only to the inmates of state penitentiaries and insane asylums. In Nevada and Washington, only people convicted of female child molestation were subject to the sterilization statutes. Most of the statutes also covered recidivists, or the so-called habitual criminals. In some cases, like Iowa, the list included almost all possible categories of the dangerous undesirables, such as "criminals, rapists, idiots, feebleminded, imbeciles, lunatics, drunkards, drug fiends, epileptics, syphilitics, moral and sexual perverts, and diseased and degenerate persons" (quoted in Hunter 1914, 515). In Iowa more than one conviction for sexual offenses was required; people convicted of "white slavery" automatically qualified for sterilization. The sterilization statutes thus became the primary weapon in the war against the threat of the feebleminded criminals. Eugenic reformers argued that the incarceration of convicted feebleminded felons was not enough, and the future threat from their descendents needed to be minimized by sterilizing them.

Though the sterilization statutes provoked challenges by scientists, politicians, religious figures, lawyers, and lay people over sixty thousand people were sterilized in the next few decades. The most famous challenge to the sterilization legislations came in Virginia in 1927 through the *Buck v. Bell* case, where the appeal against the decision of a lower court by the lawyers of Carrie Buck, a so-called feebleminded person, was upheld by the U.S. Supreme Court. Writing for the majority, Justice Oliver Wendell Holmes infamously asserted that sterilization provided for the prevention of an act of delinquency waiting to happen since it stemed from hereditary deficiencies, and "three generations of imbeciles are enough" (*Buck v. Bell*, 274 U.S. 200, 1927)

The apparent legislative success of eugenicists did not prevent criticisms from scientists, lawyers, and lay people alike about the constitutional validity of the sterilization statutes. Charles Boston, a New York lawyer and the vice president of the Society of Medical Jurisprudence, asserted that the sterilization laws violated the constitutional basis of the American legal system, as they sought to punish not a crime but the potential of a crime, thereby amounting to despotic violations of the citizenship rights (Boston 1913). Justice William O. Douglas of the U.S. Supreme Court echoed Boston in delivering the majority opinion of the court in *Skinner v. Oklahoma* when a law for sterilizing repeat offenders convicted of "moral turpitude" was overturned by the U.S. Supreme Court on the ground that it violated the equal protection clause of the Fourteenth Amendment (*Skinner v. Oklahoma*, 316 U.S. 535, U.S. Supreme Court, June 1, 1942).

While the sterilization bills have gained more infamy in history, those were only a part of series of legislative measures taken to control the so-called menace of the feebleminded since the first decade of the twentieth century. Some of these laws were directed against the propagation of hereditary feeblemindedness by restrictive marriage laws (Lindsay 1998). Michigan had banned marriage for people afflicted with certain venereal disease in 1899, and in 1905 this law was augmented by another which prevented people ever committed to an institution for epilepsy, feeblemindedness, imbecility, or insanity from being able to legally wed another person. Similar laws were passed in the Kansas, Minnesota, New Jersey, and Ohio around the same time.

A more sweeping law was passed in Indiana in 1905 that not only prevented marriage between "unfit" people, but also declared such marriages from other states to be null and void within its jurisdiction (Smith 1914). By 1939, about thirty-six states had statutes that restricted marriage among people deemed to be imbeciles or "feebleminded." Only eight states—including Alabama, Arizona, Colorado, Florida, Louisiana, Maryland, New Mexico, and Texas—did not have any laws restricting marriage on the ground of mental incompetence. Over thirty-eight states had restricted marriage on the basis of a whole host of mental conditions, including epilepsy and insanity, though not feeblemindedness per se (Wile 1939, 78).

The interaction between scientific personnel and criminal justice institutions of the period are also exemplified in the development of specialized laboratories attached to the criminal justice institutions for the mentally deficient at the state and city level. The development of these scientific-penal institutions was unique to the extent that, unlike asylums, the inmates of these institutions were convicted criminals, rather than mental health patients. At the same time, they were sent to these institutions because of their presumed psychological pathologies. Thus they were regarded as deviant both in legal and scientific sense, and served as objects of punitive sanctions as well as scientific inquiry. The idea of professional psychiatric evaluation of convicts was central to contemporary criminology and there was little divergence of opinion regarding this issue between academic criminologists and practitioners within the criminal justice system. There was a widespread belief that people with psychological disorders committed a great percentage of public order crimes. Thus, it was held that the regular prisons need to be supplemented by scientific institutions working in conjunction with the law enforcement and judicial institutions.

One of the most famous of these penal-psychological institutions was the aforementioned Psychopathic Laboratory attached to the Chicago Municipal Court under the supervision of Chief Justice Harry Olson (Willrich 1998, 2003). Within a decade of from its inception in 1914, the Chicago Psychopathic Laboratory (CPL) claimed to have examined forty thousand cases and sent about one thousand cases every year to state institutions for feebleminded (Olson 1925). Psychiatrists at the CPL administered a series of psychological tests, including the Ziehen memory test as well as the Binet-Simon test, to the offenders to detect and measure the extent of psychological defects in offenders sent for evaluation from other courts in Chicago.

It is possible to find at least three different reasons for the development of these specialized penal-scientific complexes. First, for the sake of social defense it was deemed necessary to identify and permanently segregate the defective delinquents. Second, it was generally assumed that neither normal prisons nor mental asylums were capable of adequately handling these patient-convicts since they were grouped in an intermediate category somewhere in between sane criminals and not-guilty mental patients. Putting them in the same institutional environment could have led to administrative problems of discipline and rehabilitation. Third, some people thought that identification and segregation of the defective delinquents was a humanitarian act. Since the state was responsible for the welfare of its citizens, it was especially responsible for those who were mentally disabled. Thus, on one hand, these institutions would be able to provide a safe environment, and, on the other hand, through research and experimentation scientist-jailors would be able to understand the root cause of these pathologies and devise remedial treatment regimes. Walter N. Thayer, the superintendent of *the Institution of the Defective Delinquents* in Napanoch, New York, asserted that carriers of a contagious disease were detained during an epidemic in order to be examined and cured of their maladies. There was a very similar need for indefinite imprisonment of defective delinquents in these specialized institutions for the sake of public protection (Thayer 1925).

The idea of defective delinquency provided a common meeting ground of the agenda of the contemporary scientists, criminal justice professionals, lawyers, and social reformers. It served as a point of intersection of differing institutional actors and facilitated the development of a core program for connecting the scientific and the legal definition of what was seen as a collective danger. As the belief in the innateness and heritability of criminal tendency was at the core of eugenic science and jurisprudence, it deemphasized actual criminal conduct and advocated the denial of civil, political, and social rights to the so-called undesirable people (Carey 2003).

The concept of feeblemindedness, which was at the core of the theories of defective delinquency, identified innate, heritable, and immutable mental deficiency to be the predictors of lack of moral consciousness and hence criminal behavior. However, this construction of criminal danger would give way to the idea of the psychopathology since the 1930s. A new generation of psychiatrists challenged the biological determinism inherent in the defective delinquency theory, and as an alternative posited a more fluid notion of psychological disorders that could lead to criminal behavior. The next chapter examines the origin of "dynamic" psychiatry and the identification of acquired psychological pathologies rather than intellectual or cognitive disabilities as the source of criminal danger.

NOTES

1. See Oscar McCulloch, *The Tribe of Ishmael: A Study in Social Degradation* (1888); Florence Harris Danielson and Harry Davenport, *The Hill Folk* (Cold Spring Harbor, New York: Press of the New Era, 1912); and Arthur Estabrook and Charles Davenport, *The Nam Family* (Eugenics Record Office, Memoir No. 2, 1912).
2. "Kallikak" was derived from the Greek words *Kallos* (good) and *Kakos* (bad).
3. The first eugenic sterilization bill was legislated in Pennsylvania, but it was vetoed by the governor of the state (Hunter 1914).
4. In Iowa, along with New Jersey, after the initial legislation the law was voided as unconstitutional by the state Supreme Courts. In Oregon, the first proposed sterilization law was vetoed by the Governor, and when it came up again in the statute book in 1913 it was vetoed again. In Nebraska it was vetoed in 1913 but reenacted in 1915. The California statute of 1909 included the "insane, feebleminded and criminal classes," but later it was confined only to the insane and feebleminded classes (Eugenic News, 1919 [1918]).

THREE

Origin of the Psychopathology of Crime

The previous chapter discussed the vicissitudes of eugenic thought in the scholarship on crime as well as the institutions and practices of the criminal justice system in the United States. Eugenics was a multivocal discourse and there was a degree of disagreement regarding the true nature of hereditary deviance among eugenicists, as eugenic scholars differed in their faith in the different forms of psychometric tests, and the scopes and modalities of eugenic legislations passed in America differed significantly. However, there was a general agreement on the identification of hereditary intellectual deficiency as a prime cause for crime and delinquency.

The eugenic consensus regarding the nature of deviant psyche was destabilized by the emergence of a new paradigm in criminal psychiatry (Rafter 1997b). From the 1920s, a new generation of psychiatrists began arguing for the recognition of a whole new gamut of psychiatric conditions influencing a range of criminal behavior. They did not see intellectual disability as the primary psychological cause for behavioral deviance. They distrusted the overemphasis on heredity by eugenicists, and, most importantly, they asserted the importance of psychiatric disorders stemming from early childhood experiences in determining behavioral traits. The new theories in criminal psychology brought the idea of *psychopathology* at the forefront of debates regarding the dangerousness. These ideas created the basic precepts of therapeutic justice, and firmly established the place of psychiatric expertise in the criminal justice system.

ORGANIC VS. DYNAMIC PSYCHIATRY

The concept of the "criminal insanity" was an established category in nineteenth-century psychiatry and jurisprudence in the United States. Indeed, Benjamin Rush, a signer of the Declaration of Independence and a founding figure of American psychiatry, saw insanity as the psychological correlate of underlying somatic conditions and asserted that it was a medical rather than a moral condition (Woodbury 1913). Rush, along with Pinel in France, produced some of the earliest scientific works of pathological states of the mind, or what Rush called "intellectual derangement" (Rush 1830). Rush's work on insanity, along with that of Pritchard, shaped much of the nineteenth-century psychiatric discourse in the United States. Another prominent psychiatrist of the nineteenth century, Isaac Ray, distinguished between moral mania and intellectual mania, or general insanity of sense leading to hallucinations and misrecognition of reality. For Ray, moral mania represented the pathology of the moral senses that made people unable to distinguish between right and wrong (Ray 1871).

In the latter part of the century, the term "moral insanity," much in vogue among Anglo-American psychologists and alienists, was supplanted by a new term, "psychopathic inferiority," introduced by a German psychologist, Julius L. Koch (Gough 1948; Partridge 1930). Koch's analysis located the roots of psychopathic behavior in constitutional organic aberrations (Millon et al. 1998).[1] Koch's work fell within the "organic" psychiatric tradition of the late nineteenth and early twentieth centuries that put forward a somatogenic and hereditarian theory of feeblemindedness and crime (Grob 1983). They posited that the criminal psyche is derived from organic pathologies in the brain or the nervous system and since these somatic conditions are heritable, so are criminal tendencies, which are transmitted as a character trait across generations.

The works of two European psychiatrists, Richard Von Krafft-Ebing of Austria and Emil Kraepelin of Germany, provided inspiration to contemporary organic psychiatrists in the United States. Krafft-Ebing was one of the pioneers in modern psychiatry who linked psychopathological conditions with corresponding somatic pathologies in the brain and the nervous system (1928 [1898]). Krafft-Ebing argued that the psychopaths should not be treated as regular criminals because of their moral incapacity, and therefore these individuals were subject to scientific rather than legal authority (Krafft-Ebing 1928 [1898], 500). The other, perhaps a more direct influence on American psychiatrists, was Kraepelin, who popularized the concept of *dementia praecox* coined by the German neurologist Arnold Pick.[2] Kraepelin saw it as an incurable degenerative condition of cognitive abilities as separate from emotional disorders. This condition was later renamed as *schizophrenia* by Eugen Bleuler (Bleuler 1951 [1911]).

Kraepelin further contrasted temporary mental pathologies with "constitutional psychopathology." According to him, the latter is an innate and congenital condition that is indicated by the presence of physical stigmata in the most extreme cases (Kraepelin 1981 [1907]). He argued that the fundamental symptom in the constitutional psychopathic states is that normal environmental stimuli is intensified in these individuals because of their diseased mental constitution resulting in deviant thoughts, feelings, and desires (Kraepelin 1981 [1907], 485). Thomas Szasz has identified the "invention" of *dementia praecox* as an existing morbid condition by Kraepelin and Bleuler as a foundational moment in the history of psychiatry. This was related to the attempts of medical professionals to legitimize their power as well as the evolution of asylums as penal-scientific complexes (Szasz 1961, 1988).

From the second decade of the twentieth century onward, the hereditarian theories came under increasing criticism from "dynamic" psychiatrists influenced by psychoanalytic perspectives, who emphasized life experiences and psychological traumas as major explanatory factors for behavioral deviance (Grob 1983, 1985; Lunbeck 1994; Willrich 2003). The work of Adolf Meyer, one of the most influential figures in American psychiatry, serves as an example of the transition from organic to dynamic theories. Combining his training as a neurologist in Europe and the experience of practicing as a psychiatrist in Johns Hopkins Medical School, Meyer called his approach "psychobiology," which incorporated both physiology and psychology in its study of mental disorders. Meyer argued that nerves, cells, and tissues of the brain, especially of the cerebral cortex, influence all mental activity and thus every psychological disorder is simultaneously a physiological disorder as well (Meyer 1896).

Though he did not quite give up on the somatic explanations of psychological disorders, Meyer nevertheless established the importance of studying psychological factors by emphasizing habits and early life experiences in the study of pathological behavior. In his speech hailing the opening of the Laboratory of Social Hygiene at the Bedford Hills Reformatory, he asserted that there were delinquent individuals whose pathologies were constitutional in nature, and thereby the aim of treatment should be helping them attain a degree of balance in life within the controlled environment of the institution, rather than the futile search for a complete cure. At the same time, he added that there were certain mental conditions that could actually be cured, and the patient rehabilitated to normalcy (Meyer 1952 [1916], 130).

Like many psychiatrists of his time Meyer seemed to be ambiguous about the role of heredity in psychopathology. In his presidential address to the Eugenic Research Association, he suggested that there were countless cases where behavioral pathologies could not be traced to hereditary constitutional conditions. Rather, there was a mass of evidence suggesting causes of "ontogenetic nature" which were often obscured by picking out a few selective factors of eugenic significance (Meyer 1952 [1917], 304–5). While he did not completely reject the role of heredity, he advocated scientific skepticism about the extent of its influence.

Perhaps the most important works in the psychological tradition in contemporary American criminology came from William Healy and Edith Spaulding (Petrunick 1982; Rafter 1997b). Healy was trained as a psychiatrist, and became famous for his work as president of the Juvenile Psychopathic Institute, affiliated with the Juvenile Court in Chicago (Willrich 2003). The Juvenile Psychopathic Institute grew out of a research committee on delinquency convened by Judge Merritt Pinkney of the Cook County Juvenile Court, and was formally established in 1909 by a group of Chicago-area philanthropists and social workers (Jones 1999). Healy's first major work on crime, titled *The Individual Delinquent* (1915), was a report of the one thousand case studies that Healy conducted in the Juvenile Psychopathic Institute.

While he was once a member of the American Eugenic Society, Healy had moved considerably from hereditary theories of crime by the time he started his work in the Juvenile Psychopathic Institute. He presented a multilevel causal theory of crime, embracing social and psychological conditions as primary causative factors. While he did not completely give up the concept of constitutional psychopathology, according to him it constituted a very small portion of the sample of his study and was thereby less important than environmental and acquired psychological problems.

Healy made a strong case for individualized studies of crime as opposed to making generalized causal theories of heritability of crime since he held that something as complex as human behavior cannot be reduced to monocausal explanations. Twenty different categories, including physiological, psychological, and environmental conditions, constituted his list of causative factors for delinquency. While his overall scientific agenda was against privileging any specific groups of causative factors, he seemed to put relatively strong emphasis on premature development of adult sexual instincts as predictive of delinquent behavior (Healy 1915). According to him, as precocious sexual development came without the maturation of the superego, a corollary of attaining psychological adulthood, this could lead to confusion of moral instincts. Also, repression and subconscious mental conflict, stemming from sexual causes but not limited to it, played a major role in producing delinquent behavior. He found that most mental conflicts among his sample of female patients were related to the sexual problems, while the reasons are more varied among the male population and included issues of parentage, social experiences, and family relationships (Healy 1915, 353). However, while this suggests a proto-Freudian perspective, Healy was ambivalent about the efficacy of Freudianism in understanding delinquency. He claimed not to be convinced by the determinism inherent in Freud's analysis that reduced all forms of psychological conditions to repression of sexual desires. Rather, he said, deep emotional disturbances were caused by a multitude of reasons, and the resultant anger, hopelessness, or moral weaknesses might result in delinquent careers (Healy 1915, 120).[3]

Drawing on Meyer's work, Healy created the category of psychic constitutional inferiority (PCI). He defined PCI as recognized by chronic abnormal behavioral conditions that cannot be attributed to insanity, neuroses, or mental defects, which are distinguished by the presence of structural or functional anomalies (Healy 1915, 575). Carefully drawing the distinction between people with PCI and those who acquired mental debilities later in life due to traumatic experience or environmental conditions, Healy claimed that the PCI patients were not born as delinquents but possessed a psyche characterized by "weakness of will, inability to cope with the social demand of self-restraint, the peculiar feeling of impotence," which made them susceptible to delinquent behavior. This, coupled with unwholesome family life and other environmental conditions, could turn people with PCI into criminals (Healy 1915, 581). Though he did not specify the actual numbers, it appears that this class was a very small portion of his sample (Rafter 1997b).

As is evident from the construction of the category of PCI, Healy did not completely give up the possibility of inherent psychopathology. However, in his overall analytic schema constitutional pathologies played a very small role, and he put forward a strong critique of theories of heritable criminality: "Apart from the researches on the inheritance of various mental and nervous defects or aberrations that are so frequently correlated with delinquency, we find nothing in the least convincing" (Healy 1915, 141). In conclusion of *The Individual Delinquent,* he argued this more forcefully by saying that based on the research there was no valid reason to believe in the existence of a class of "born criminals." Certain individuals with psychological defects, especially if they were raised in unwholesome environments, might be regarded as possessing "secondarily criminal dispositions." But it would be very difficult to demonstrate the causal primacy of heritable factors over environmental ones in these cases (Healy 1915, 141).

Drawing from their research in the Juvenile Psychopathic Institute, Healy and his colleague Edith Spaulding published an article around the same time that *The Individual Delinquent* was released, which in spite of all customary caveats concluded that the relation between heredity and criminal tendencies could not be scientifically proved (Spaulding and Healy 1914). In their complete statistical data on the topic of inheritance, Healy and Spaulding found that a majority of the cases of delinquency did not show any possible correlation with heredity. However, they did find, in a percentage of the total cases, parents and grandparents with mental disorders. But Healy warned against drawing hasty conclusions from this data by saying that there was little evidence to suggest that delinquency was caused or transmitted by heredity in cases where such behavior was present within various members of the same family across generations. Most studies revealed that these individuals shared similar environmental conditions and consequently might be more influenced by the latter (Healy 1915, 141). Thus, Healy contended that the presence of multiple delinquents in the same family across generations could be a result of unwholesome socialization, and therefore was explained better by the insights of social psychology rather than genetics (Healy and Healy 1915). Healy also argued that stigmata or physical deformity was present in some of the cases, but that it could not be scientifically connected to delinquency. Physical deformity was correlated with mental defects as well as nutritional and environmental conditions, but that was not necessarily predictive of deviant or criminal behavior. Similarly, he did not find a strong correlation between feeblemindedness and crime, as only 10 percent of his sample showed intellectual incapacity and more than two-thirds of the sample showed no symptom of mental abnormality (Healy 1915, 146).

Based on her own research of the inmates of Bedford Hills Reformatory in New York, Edith Spaulding expressed doubts about the efficacy of intelligence tests, particularly Binet-Simon tests, in the detection of criminal tendencies (Rafter 1997b; Spaulding 1915). The alternative, according to her, was a more holistic approach that would include a comprehensive case study method embracing physiological, psychological, social, and psychiatric evaluations (Spaulding 1915). In a more detailed analysis of Bedford Hills inmates, Spaulding further added that she failed to see the existence of any physical marks signifying degeneracy and delinquency, and she put more emphasis on emotions, experiences, and impulses, rather than constitutional or organic conditions as explanatory factors of delinquency (Spaulding 1923). While Spaulding and Healy did not categorically rule out the possibility of intergenerational transmission of delinquent traits, they nevertheless challenged this pivotal postulate of eugenic psychiatry by showing the almost insurmountable barrier to the verification of the hereditarian assumption. They also emphasized the possibility of what is normally regarded as heredity itself being a dependent variable to environment—that great anathema of the eugenicists.

The dynamic perspective thus assumed a much more fluid nature of the human psyche, which is molded by existential and environmental factors, and that delinquent as well as nonpathological traits are acquired through the life experience of the individual rather than biologically inherited from previous generations. The process of detection of the psychological pathologies differed crucially from the theories of defective delinquency as intelligence tests gave way to psychoanalytic methods. The point of psychopathology was not to identify poorly developed mental faculties but rather the perversions of the subconscious or the unconscious mind that result from experience, lack of socialization, or childhood traumas. The psychotic, rather than the feebleminded individual, emerged as the new agent of criminal danger. A series of legislation passed in some states since the 1930s sought to control a subset of this risky population—the so-called sexual psychopaths.

THE SEXUAL PSYCHOPATH LAWS: PSYCHIATRIC EXPERTISE AND LEGAL DANGEROUSNESS

The so-called Briggs Law of Massachusetts (1921) was one of the earliest and most comprehensive laws regarding the assessment of criminal danger.[4] It was drafted by and passed at the initiative of L. Vernon Briggs, a psychiatrist and one-time president of the Massachusetts Psychiatric Society (Overholser 1934). The Briggs Law established mandatory psychiatric examinations of all habitual offenders and persons accused of serious felonies (Glueck 1928). An increasing number of cases were reported in the next decade. Whereas eighty-four such examinations took place on average every year between 1921 and 1926, by 1930 this number had jumped to more than three hundred (Overholser 1932, 416). The Briggs Law was not directed at any special category of psychopathological behavior, but it did establish the importance of psychiatric expertise in the judicial system. Indeed, it was seen by some as being a harbinger of the future when laws would do more than punish on the basis of the mechanical interpretation of criminal statutes. Instead, the scientific knowledge of experts would offer a rational solution to the problem of crimes committed by offenders suffering from psychological maladies. These individuals were seen as being incapable of using moral judgment yet not unfit to stand trial for reasons of insanity as established by the M'Naughten rule (Glueck 1927).[5]

In 1937, Michigan passed the first sexual psychopathy legislation, but it was later found to be unconstitutional by the Michigan Supreme Court. The original law targeted a person convicted of a sexual offense. These offenses ranged from public indecency to rape, committed by a person who was not insane but diagnosed as suffering from psychiatric disorder with sexual deviant tendencies, and regarded as a threat to public safety. The law authorized the court to call in medical professionals, including psychiatrists, to examine such a person after conviction, and if that person was diagnosed with a psychopathic personality, the court might commit that person to an appropriate state hospital for an indeterminate period. In 1938, in a case resulting from the law, *People v. Frontczak*, the Michigan Supreme Court invalidated the legislation by a very narrow majority on the grounds of violating due process rights accorded to every individual under the Michigan constitution for criminal cases, especially with regard to the indeterminate confinement (Jackson 1939, 621–22).[6]

Illinois passed the first valid sexual psychopath law, the Act to Provide for the Commitment and Detention of Criminal Sexual Psychopathic Persons, in the same year that the Michigan statute was invalidated. The Illinois statute went further than the Michigan law in its objective of controlling the public danger posed by the psychopathic sex offenders. The law stated that an individual with history of mental disorder leading to sexual deviance, but not otherwise diagnosed as clinically insane or feebleminded, was the "sexual psychopathic person." It authorized the district attorney to file a writ with the court if a person charged with a criminal offense (not necessarily sexual in nature) was suspected of being a sexual psychopath. The court would then appoint two psychiatrists to make a diagnosis. Once the psychiatric evaluation was submitted, the court would convene a jury to determine the sufficiency of evidence of the existence of psychopathic tendencies. If the jury determined such a condition, the person would be incarcerated in the psychiatric division of the Illinois State Penitentiary. The final verdict was to be determined by a second jury, who would judge if the person had truly recovered from the malady. Then the person would be tried and punished for the original offense (Jackson 1939). Following a challenge to constitutionality of the statute in 1944, it was upheld by the Illinois Supreme Court, which asserted that the state legislature had the authority to promulgate a law that classified psychopathic individuals as separate from ordinary offenders in a criminal case, and the statute took into consideration the need for the proper treatment of these individuals as well as ensuring public safety.[7]

Certain legal assumptions underlying the very idea of psychopathology typified the sexual psychopath legislations passed in the 1930s. Both the Michigan and Illinois laws distinguished psychopathic individuals as being a distinct category not subsumed under the general legal prescriptions regarding insanity or feeblemindedness. These also highlighted the presence of a history of such a condition as past behavior was seen as a predictor of future action by both scientifically and legally establishing the "propensity" of deviant behavior (Jackson 1939).

Within the next few years, several other states passed similar legislation. Among all the state laws on mental deficiency and psychopathology, the New Jersey statute went the furthest in its classificatory schema. "Psychopathic delinquent" was classified in three categories: "subnormal mentality coupled with mental instability," "intelligent offenders of unstable personality," and "the psychopathic offenders of average or above average intelligence" (Robinson 1933). In California, the statute authorized the court to decide if there was probable cause to believe that a person convicted of any offense regardless of its nature was a sexual psychopath (Hacker and Frym 1955). The Minnesota statute (1939) provided an elaborate definition of psychopathic personality, including emotional instability, impulsiveness, lack of judgment, and irresponsibility of conduct (Reinhardt and Fisher 1949). Unlike the Illinois law, the Minnesota statute did not apply to any accused in a criminal case, but to any individuals in the state who might be perceived as a threat because of deviant sexual desires that rendered them incapable of exercising their judgment in a competent way (FPF 1948). Similarly, the District of Columbia defined sexual psychopaths as individuals accused of repeated acts of sexual "misconduct" yet not showing any sign of insanity. These individuals could not control their urges and thus represented a threat to other people who may suffer from mental or physical injury (Reinhardt and Fisher 1949).

While these laws were passed to control the "dangerous" sexual offenders, the vagueness of the legal definitions led to an expansion of the target to cover all kinds of sexual offenses. Some contemporary legal scholars argued that a number of so-called sex offenders were accused or convicted of offenses that might be seen as morally offensive by many but were by no means a threat to the general public, as they took place among consenting adults, or acts conducted in private that did not cause any harm to any other person. Added to this, these individuals faced long prison terms without any form of therapeutic facilities. Thus, less severe punishment, including probation or shorter sentences, might provide a better way of dealing with the problem (Ploscowe 1960, 223). Edwin Sutherland argued that though these laws were limited in their actual application, they were quite dangerous from a constitutional point of view. Moreover, they raised serious questions regarding the monopoly of psychiatric expertise in criminal cases. Without discounting the scientific validity of the practice of psychiatrists, he argued that other disciplines, such as social workers and sociologists, as well as psychologists, needed to be utilized with equal importance given the multidimensional nature of human conduct, especially those that violate moral and legal codes that underlie the social order (Sutherland 1950).

SCIENTIFIC CONSTRUCTION OF PSYCHOPATHOLOGY

The term psychopathology was well established in scientific and legal circles by the late 1940s. The American Medico-Psychological Association used the term for the first time in their *Statistical Manual for the Use of Hospitals for Mental Diseases* in 1934.[8] Hervey Cleckley offered one of the most comprehensive contemporary definitions of psychopathy. He listed sixteen conditions, including pathologic egocentrism, lack of remorse for conduct, and history of antisocial behavior, in identifying potential psychopaths (Cleckley 1941).

However, in most of the contemporary discussions of the topic, the term "psychopathic" personality was used in a rather expansive sense. In most cases, it included a whole host of psychological maladies thought to be linked with criminal behavior, much to the consternation of some scholars who criticized the lack of definitional clarity (Thornton 1951). Since the early 1950s onward, some psychiatrists challenged the very idea of psychopathic personality on the grounds of being overextended at the cost of its analytical value. Bernard Glueck, a supervising psychiatrist of the Sing Sing prison and the director of a research project by the New York Department of Mental Hygiene on offenders incarcerated for sexual or other offenses in Sing Sing, reported that the label "psychopath" as a distinct category simplified the enormous complexity of the mental and emotional disorders linked with crime. According to Glueck, a majority of the offenders could not be classified as psychopaths, since they did not show the classic symptoms of psychopathic behavior—the lack of anxiety and guilt: "We have abandoned psychopathic personality as a diagnosis, in our studies on these men, and are placing most of the individuals so diagnosed on previous examinations in the schizophrenic group" (Glueck 1954, 125).

Glueck argued that the common identification of schizophrenia as insanity obfuscates the fact that many patients displaying schizophrenic tendencies or reactions were not legally insane and hence seen as morally culpable for their actions. Yet the causes of their crime, unconscious motivations and desires, remained beyond their control and henceforth they could not be seen as responsible in the strict sense of the term. This problematized the whole conception of free will and legal responsibility enshrined in the M'Naughten Rule, which until then was the central precept of establishing criminal guilt. Thus Glueck argued that in situations like this, the purpose of punishment should not be retribution, but rather incapacitation and rehabilitation. Rather than punishing according to a set legal formula, the courts should sentence the offenders to a treatment facility where scientific professionals would diagnose the problem, and prescribe a treatment regime. The length of the sentence should be determined by how well the inmate responded to treatment and was cured of their mental disorders (Glueck 1954, 130).

Another contemporary specialist on sexual deviance, Benjamin Karpman, did not consider sexual psychopath to be a useful concept at all, and advocated the use of the concepts of *paraphiliac neuroses* or *neurotic perversity* instead (1941, 1951, 1954): "The paraphiliac fails to channel their desires according to the social conventions, due to improper development or maturation of their sexual instincts, which leads to aberrant and abnormal sexual activity" (1951, 186). He argued that as a form of neurosis, paraphilia was present in varying degrees among a wide section of the population. In some cases, patients managed to control their impulses, and in some cases it manifested itself into a wide variety of symptoms, including depression, feelings of inferiority, and hysterical convulsions. This way, paraphilia was very similar to other forms of neurosis in its origin, except that it manifested itself in overtly sexualized behavior. In a number of cases the behavioral urges stemming from the condition were beyond the control of the individual and violated social as well as legal norms, and it is these individuals who were branded as sexual psychopaths.

In Karpman's view, the most important characteristic of psychopathic behavior was the lack of any guilt because of a weak conscience or superego. This led to the absence of a sense of moral responsibility, and the inability to consider the consequences, excessive selfishness in one's interpersonal relationships, and aggressiveness beyond the conscious control of the individual. This aggressiveness was also manifested in violent outbursts motivated by unconscious sexual impulses, though not overtly sexual in nature. Karpman claimed that in spite of the contemporary advances in dynamic psychiatry, there was little knowledge regarding the etiology of sexual deviance. Research showed that it was not hereditary since a significant number of these individuals did not come from a family with a history of sexually perverse behavior. In a very small number of cases, they were linked to congenital disorders such as encephalitis, but most patients did not show any evidence of somatic defects. Early childhood experiences and repressed sexuality certainly played a role, but the exact origins of such conditions had not yet been diagnosed. He was critical of the sexual psychopath laws since he argued that laws made a simple distinction between right and wrong without recognizing the subtle variations that existed between various psychiatric conditions. Also, the purpose of legal sanctions was punishment of misdeeds, which did not serve the purpose when it came to these crimes since the offender did not have much control over his or her behavior and thereby could not be reformed by penal sanctions. They should be subject to control of psychiatric professionals rather than incarcerated along with common criminals.

However, the important legal issue here was the dual status of these individuals as offenders and patients, and the determination of the relative control of medical or penal authorities in determining when and how they would be allowed to rejoin the society once they were declared "safe," and allowed to be released from custody. The judgment of psychopathology was based on a fundamental ambiguity, which stemmed from both the nature and the objectives of the respective institutions of psychiatry and law. While the former diagnosed the conditions that prompted individuals to undertake certain courses of actions, the latter focused on judgment of a specific offense. Thus, psychiatric aspects of law enforcement may have focused more on rehabilitation or incapacitation based on the scientific judgment of the mental state of the offender. But judicial and penal institutions may have focused on retribution and restoration as well. A common refrain in public discourse has been that sentencing people convicted of a serious act of harm to a psychiatric facility does not deliver justice to the victims and thereby represents a serious miscarriage of justice (Petrunick 1982). The sexual psychopath statutes, some of the earliest examples of a hybrid between science and law, did not clarify this central contradiction between the respective jurisdictions of the institutions involved in enforcement. Only Indiana, Michigan, and New Hampshire stipulated that commitment to a psychiatric facility also disposed of the criminal charge.

For most of the first half of the twentieth century, psychiatric expertise in the criminal justice system centered on clinical assessment of individual convicts in order to assess the nature and extent of the danger they posed to the community. This was very much a product of the discourse of individualized justice that arose in the early years of the twentieth century. Individualization was seen as a cornerstone of a democratic justice system to the extent that it was directed at treating every criminal case as unique, and designing a penal sanction that would fit the gravity of the offense and the nature of the offender with a very clear rehabilitative ideal through the use of indeterminate sentence and therapeutic measures within the penal system. The enhanced role and influence of psychiatrists in the court and the prison system was rooted in the belief dating back to the Progressive era that scientific expertise was an ally of good governance, and the enlightened authority of science would serve the objectives of the justice system by studying, analyzing, and reforming human nature. So the psychiatrist in the judicial and the penal system assumed the combined roles of a neutral analyst and an agent of social control at the same time. This became the basis of civil commitment of psychiatric patients throughout the 1950s and 1960s, extending beyond sexual offenses and covering a wide range of threats to public safety.

NOTES

1. Koch did account for some psychopathic conditions that do not have a hereditary organic basis, and could be caused by a moral debility acquired from external causes (Wetzell 2000).

2. The term was first used by Morel as *démence précoce*, or "early dementia," in 1853. Pick used the Latin form that became popular among the late nineteenth-century psychiatrists.

3. It is interesting to note that both Healy's contemporaries and later researchers have commented on the ambivalence inherent in Healy's theories. Kathleen Jones finds it puzzling that despite the apparent strong emphasis on environmental factors, he warned against overemphasizing it at the cost of other causative factors (Jones 1999, 47). Similarly, John T. MacCurdy, while praising the book as an important contribution to criminology, bemoans the lack of general theory of delinquency (MacCurdy 1916, 361). In defense of Healy, however, one can say that given his methodology and the focus on individuation of subjects his goal was not theory-building, but trying to understand particular cases in all their complexities.

4. Massachusetts established some of the earliest instances of involuntary commitment of people deemed to be a threat to public safety (Robinson 1933). The Massachusetts Acts and Resolves (1911) created a special category of offenders found to be

suffering from a mental condition that made them prone to delinquent behavior. The law ordered that these people be put in the custody of the newly established Department of Defective Delinquents since these individuals could not be confined in ordinary prison, insane asylums, or institutions for truants or the feebleminded (Commonwealth of Massachusetts 1922).

5. The M'Naughten Rule defined legal insanity as the incapacity of distinguishing between right and wrong.

6. The minority opinion written by Justice Butzel argued that due process rights were not germane to the statute, as it was very similar to other statutes authorizing confinement of "these unfortunate and dangerous persons" for the sake of public safety and the welfare of these individuals. Thus, it was not any different from the defective delinquent legislations passed by most states, including Michigan (Jackson 1939, 623).

7. Since the invalidation of the Michigan statute, some state laws were legislated within the purview of civil laws in order to circumvent the due process challenges that might have arisen out of proceedings within criminal codes (FPF 1948, 878).

8. When the American Psychological Association published the first *Diagnostic and Statistical Manual* (DSM-I) in 1952, the term "psychopathology" was replaced by a new term: "sociopathic personality." In 1980, DSM-III introduced the term "anti-social personality disorder." In recent times, some psychologists have called for a revision of this category. One of the major criticisms is the break with the more clinical definitions of psychopathic behavior and choosing to focus on a broad set of behavioral patterns without any consideration to the origin of these conditions (Hare et al. 1991). Additionally, these are generally a set of fixed behavioral indicators whose presence suggests the existence of antisocial personality behavior to the analysts. However, the mere presence of certain behavioral indicators does not provide the analytical leverage to understand the nature and etiology of the underlying causes of the disorder. Indeed, similar behavioral traits may result from a whole host of social and psychological factors and, conversely, the same causative factors may result in a variety of behavioral forms (Hare et al. 1991).

FOUR

The Advent of Actuarial Justice

While the relation between psychological maladies and crime has been postulated since the days of eugenics in the United States, it received a boost in the late 1960s. In this era, dangerousness was no longer conceptualized as stemming from intellectual deficiencies or sexual psychopathology as was the case in the recent past. The clause of dangerousness was widely used in involuntary commitment of mental patients in the name of preventive detention. Historically, custodial control of mental patients has been informed by the doctrine of *parens patrie*, or the patrimonial authority of the state over the lives of the citizens for their own good (Mihm 1954). The dangerousness legislations, however, were informed more by the principles of social defense, and the right of the state to use coercive power in order to safeguard from potential harm that can befall innocents from the actions of individuals with a predilection for violent behavior.

Many proponents of these measures saw them as serving public good by incapacitating the most violent of offenders. The 1973 Task Force for Corrections of the National Advisory Commission on Criminal Justice Standards and Goals recommended that persistent offenders or the dangerous criminals should be given the most stringent of sentences as psychiatric diagnosis or their previous record indicated that these individuals would be a significant threat to the society. It was argued that the authority to sentence individuals posing a danger to society might allow the legislatures to consider shorter sentences for nonviolent offenders. This would alleviate a significant burden to the prison system (Morris and Miller 1985). Clinical assessment of offenders was thus seen as an essential tool for the rational administration of the criminal justice system.

The reign of psychiatric expertise was not without its detractors both within and outside the criminal justice system. One of the unique legal characteristics of the dangerousness statutes was that the guilt or punishment was not determined by the jury or a judge, but the judgment of a scientific professional (Dershowitz 1969). Additionally, penal judgments based on the concept of dangerousness were governed by the potential, rather than any actual offense committed by an individual. Penal decisions based on clinical diagnosis of danger implied privileging the specialist knowledge over the principle of *actus reus*, seen by some as being fundamentally against the judicial and penal principles of a democratic society.

DANGER AND DISSENT

One of the first legal challenges against the dangerousness statutes came with *Baxstrom v. Herold* (Simon 2005a; Steadman and Cocozza 1974, 1978). Many of the so-called criminally insane inmates in the New York State Penitentiary System facility in Dannemora, New York, were held captive past their original sentence as they were diagnosed as being a danger to society or themselves. The U.S. Supreme Court overturned the decision of the New York Supreme Court, and opined that the incarceration beyond the length of the original sentence is a violation of due process rights, and close to one thousand of these inmates were released back into the community, or committed to psychiatric facilities run by the New York Department of Mental Hygiene following regular civil commitment procedures (U.S. Supreme Court 1966).

Over the next two decades, a number of Supreme Court judgments revisited issues raised by *Baxstrom v. Herold*, and ruled against indefinite commitment of people deemed to be dangerous. In *Jackson v. Indiana* the Supreme Court ruled that the indefinite incarceration in a mental institution of people deemed unfit to stand trial for mental incompetence is a violation of the equal protection clause: "Such a defendant cannot be held more than the reasonable period of time necessary to determine whether there is a substantial probability that he will attain competency in the foreseeable future. If it is determined that he will not, the State must either institute civil proccedings applicable to the commitment of those not charged with a crime, or release the defendant" (U.S. Supreme Court 1972).

The question of what constituted danger was the central issue in *Addington v. Texas* (Slobogin 1984). Frank Addington's contention that his indefinite commitment in a mental institution violated his constitutional rights was upheld by the Texas Court of Appeals but overturned by the Texas Supreme Court. The U.S. Supreme Court granted his certiorari request while overturning the appeal:

> The individual's liberty interest in the outcome of a civil commitment proceeding is of such weight and gravity, compared with the state's interests in providing care to its citizens who are unable, because of emotional disorders, to care for themselves and in protecting the community from the dangerous tendencies of some who are mentally ill, that due process requires the state to justify confinement by proof more substantial than a mere preponderance of the evidence. (U.S. Supreme Court 1979)

The decision also stated that, given the uncertainties of psychiatric diagnoses, the state should not be expected to employ the "beyond reasonable doubt" standard of proof as these might endanger innocent citizens and pose barriers to people in need of treatment.

The debates over dangerousness also included the issue of the responsibility of the psychiatric professional to potential victims and the society at large. The diagnosis and treatment of a patient was generally covered by confidentiality privilege central to the code of ethics in the medical profession. However, some argued that if the patient was diagnosed with a condition that may result in violence or harm to a third party, the psychiatric professional had a special responsibility to warn potential victims of the patient (Fleming and Maximov 1974). This view was partly influenced by the critiques of psychiatry in the 1960s, which saw psychiatric professionals as agents of social control. Thus, Fleming and Maximov provided a more libertarian solution to the problem in arguing that warnings of possible threats precluded the necessity of incarcerating mental patients who were diagnosed with conditions that may prompt violent behavior (Stone 1976). At the same time, it also problematized the question of medical liability and malpractice by arguing that therapeutic practice, especially in the psychological context, involved a degree of medical control over the patient. This control necessitated the assumption of responsibility over the conduct of the patient under therapy to a large extent. Fleming and Maximov cited the example of cases where hospitals had been held liable for negligence when the patients under their care caused harm to other individuals.

This issue came to prominence in the 1975 decision of the California Supreme Court in *Tarasoff v. The Regents of the University of California* (Dix 1980). The *Tarasoff* decision held that if the therapist's diagnosis reveals the threat of imminent harm to another person, he/she is obliged to take precautionary steps including but not limited to informing the potential victim or law enforcement authorities. One of the problems of the decision, as pointed out by the dissenting opinion of Justice Clark, was that this might have a serious adverse effect on the guarantee of confidentiality of patient records. Consequently, people in need of psychiatric help might be less likely to see a doctor, which would not only affect the patient but also society and potential victims (Stone 1976).

SCIENTIFIC CHALLENGES TO CLINICAL ASSESSMENT OF DANGER

Perhaps the strongest challenge to psychiatric assessment of dangerousness came from an unexpected source—psychiatrists themselves. Since the mid-1970s onward a series of research projects questioned the veracity of the diagnoses made by the psychiatrists regarding future dangerousness of patients and inmates. These cast serious doubts on the conventional wisdom in criminal psychiatry over the previous quarter century (Simon 2005a). These challenges hinged on the contention that research did not provide necessary and sufficient proof regarding mental illness as the key predictor of violence.

A core contention of the critics was the conceptual amorphousness and lack of specificity of the very idea of dangerousness (Pfohl 1978; Rennie 1978; Steadman 1976; Steadman and Cocozza 1978; Warren 1979). While the law called for the internment of a person found to be dangerous to the safety of others, there was little clarity regarding the specific nature of offenses that would indicate future potential for crime as well. The potential vastness of this category went against the scientific precision needed for prediction. In an early critique of the conceptual expanse of the idea, Goldstein and Katz argued that the category "dangerous behavior" was overextended to the level of losing all specificity (Goldstein and Katz 1960, 235). The principle of dangerousness was remarkably elastic and this came in the way of rigorous scientific operationalization.

Another major problem with the psychiatric prediction of dangerous behavior was the lack of consensus regarding the predictors. This was partially due to the conceptual amorphousness of the very idea of danger, and the lack of certainty regarding the necessity and sufficiency of these factors in the commission of violent acts. MacDonald's study of one hundred patients incarcerated in the Colorado Psychopathic Hospital for threats of violence demonstrated that while a small percentage of these individuals indeed committed acts of violence against others or themselves, over 90 percent of the sample had not commited any aggressive acts (MacDonald 1967). Similarly, in a 1971 study of a group of juvenile murderers, Malmquist posited the existence of certain premonitory signs as predictors of violent behavior, including certain behavior changes before the commission of a violent act such as emotional turbulence, "object loss," and hypochondria. At the same time, he conceded that these were prevalent among a range of people who did not commit violent acts whatsoever (Malmquist 1971). In the 1960s, clinical practitioners also adopted Hellman and Blackman's theory of the childhood history of arson and cruelty as predictors of future violence (Hellman and Blackman 1966). However, subsequent research showed no consistent difference between control groups and mental patients with a record of violence in terms of these factors (Diamond 1974).

The methodological problem that plagued most of the early studies of dangerousness was that most of these were based on a preselected group of individuals accused or convicted of acts of violence. Thus, though some of these studies were based on relatively large samples, in most cases these did not include control groups to test for the validity of the identified factors. Many scholars questioned the psychiatric wisdom on the idea, and argued that the assessment of danger was not a value-neutral and objective scientific decision in spite of all the claims to that effect (Ennis and Litwack 1974; Petrunik 1982; Steadman and Cocozza 1974). Thus, in some cases these explained more about the institutional practices of psychiatry and criminal justice, rather than judgment of human nature. Thornberry and Jacoby argued that the fact of overprediction of probability of violent behavior among mental patients was neither accidental nor the product of honest mistakes. Rather, it was the hallmark of the way society dealt with individuals labeled as mentally unstable (Thornberry and Jacoby 1979). Similarly, some argued that the business of prediction served the political function of reducing the multiple dimensions of action to psychiatric pathologies, and thereby provided a very limited understanding of the complexities of the human condition (Pfohl 1978).

The fact that violent behavior, much like other kinds of behavior, stems from the complex combination of factors, many of which are not psychiatric in nature, was not given due credence by the conventional processes of assessing danger. The very understanding of danger as a psychiatric or medical category itself was open to question (Levinson and Ramsey 1979). Psychiatric assessment of danger was not that different from other ways of imposing guilt by suspicion—only that it was rendered with an aura of scientific finality by the very people whose professions benefited significantly in the process. Thus, the scientificity of the practices of dangerousness could be problematized by investigations into the institutional processes of assigning danger from a constructivist perspective, which would highlight the ways in which the careers and professions of clinical practitioners are instrumental in the diagnostic process (Conrad and Dinitz 1977; Pfohl 1978; Warren 1979; Webster et al. 1982).

The dangerousness legislations were based on the assumption that the potential of future harm could be accurately predicted by statistical or psychological methods. However, this ran the risk of the possibility of overprediction and the "false positive" diagnosis of dangerousness, which might result in the indefinite incarceration of the people who were, in effect, not "dangerous" (Dershowitz 1974, 1978; Morris 1974). A number of studies since the 1970s found that most predictions of future violence contain a high percentage of false positives. A ten-year study (1962–1972) intended to conclusively prove the predictive accuracy of the clinical methods undertaken at the Bridgewater Institution of Massachusetts among people sent for assessment under the Massachusetts Sexually Dangerous Persons Act (1947) focused on eighty-two people who were released by the court upon the recommendation of the clinical staff, and forty-nine people who were released against the recommendations of the staff (Kozol et al. 1972; Petrunik 1982). Kozol and his colleagues claimed to follow a rigorous system of assessment that included a whole set of factors accepted as predictors of psychopathic behavior (Kozol et al. 1972, 379). Though the study claimed a high degree of accuracy of assessment made by the clinical staff of the institution, a very high percentage of false positive diagnosis cast doubts on their claim. Other researchers assessing this claim argued that the study did reasonably well in diagnosing true negatives, or people who did not commit any crimes after release, but did poorly in the diagnosis of future danger, which belied the claim of overall methodological soundness of the diagnostic procedures. Doubts about the ability to conclusively distinguish between true and false positives in predicting the propensity to violence remained (Stone 1976). Monahan claimed that contemporary psychiatric assessments of dangerousness had the tendency to overestimate and consequently falsely diagnose a very high percentage of people to be dangerous. This cast serious doubts about the basic methodological assumptions behind the diagnoses (Monahan 1978, 1981).

Similarly, two other psychiatrists who have been long critical of clinical assessment of danger, Joseph Steadman and Henry Cocozza, claimed that the trust in psychiatric expertise in the criminal justice system might be misplaced given its inability to make accurate predictions of dangerousness. They also added that the factor that may have some predictive value, as they found in their own study, was the seriousness of the alleged offense of the defendant. However, they argued that this too by itself is not a persuasive predictive factor, as proven by other studies on recidivism. Evidence suggested that in most cases, the predictions were based on factors that did not require any psychiatric expertise to identify. Psychiatrists also reported the pressure to make a diagnosis, and given the potential severe consequences of making a false negative diagnosis and the responsibility of preventing violent offenses, there may be a tendency to err on the side of caution. Given the fact that psychiatric assessments are taken as the final scientific judgment of a person's nature, and that the persons mistakenly diagnosed as a threat to society have little recourse, the consequences are much less severe for a false positive diagnosis. This provides the society with convenient scapegoats who can be labeled and demonized as psychopaths and thereby not make any enduring reforms to the very functioning of the society that produces these individuals in the first place (Steadman and Cocozza 1978).

Steadman undertook one of the most exhaustive surveys of patient/inmates freed by the *Baxstrom* decision. In the five-year period since the

Baxstrom decision, a total of 967 patients were transferred to civil mental hospitals and only twenty-six were returned to maximum-security facilities. This group included fifteen patients sent from civilian hospitals, and eleven who were rearrested after release into the community. The latter group was split in half between persons found incompetent to stand trial and persons convicted of a crime and sent back as psychologically deranged criminals. Steadman found that two factors distinguished these twenty-six individuals from the rest of the original *Baxstrom* releases—their relatively younger age and prior arrest record (Steadman 1973).

Around the same time, both the American Psychiatric Association and the American Psychological Association declared that contemporary methodologies of predicting dangerousness lack scientific reliability (APA 1974; Menzies et al. 1985; Slobogin 1984, 2006). These came around the same time as the series of superior court decisions that began with the *Baxstrom* case opening up the possibility of procedural challenges and lawsuits against forensic psychiatrists potentially threatening the reputation, integrity, and autonomy of the profession. These criticisms amounted to a serious scientific challenge to the modus operandi of assessing criminal danger, given the fact that some of these were coming from psychiatrists involved in the very processes of determining dangerousness. At the same time, many of these scholars and practitioners who acknowledged the problems and shortcomings of clinical assessment still believed in the necessity of the very endeavor of risk assessment, and thereby sought to devise more sophisticated predictive instruments that might yield more accurate results (Menzies et al. 1985; Monahan 1981; Prins 1981; Shah 1981).

One of the inherent problems with psychiatric risk assessment was the medicalized definition of the problem and the consequent overreliance on the clinical methods of analysis. Psychiatric experts overemphasized psychological and psychopathological variables without analyzing a whole host of structural and contextual factors that are essential in the prediction of antisocial behavior. Assessment and prediction of violence or dangerous behavior, very much like any other kind of human behavior, is inherently complex, as human personality is the product of multiple individual, social, situational, and interpersonal variables rather than an innate, unchanging entity. Thus, rather than individualized clinical assessments the analysis of this multitude of contributing factors necessitated the use of multivariate statistics (Menzies et al. 1985). The American Psychiatric Association endorsed this view and concluded that dangerousness is a product of multiple factors, and cannot just be seen as an individual psychological condition (APA 1974).

Also in question was the very role of psychiatric expertise in the process of the analysis and prediction of violence. Studies had demonstrated that people without much clinical training or experience could make predictions that might be quite accurate (Menzies et al. 1985; Steadman and

Cocozza 1974; Thornberry and Jacoby 1979). This was also linked with the problems of diagnostic miscalculations of individual psychiatric assessors and the lack of uniform standards across the society that could make the process more transparent and reliable. Thus there was also the perceived need for standardization of assessment instruments and procedures. These created the intellectual context for the formation of various actuarial instruments, and the increasing emphasis on the language of risk, rather than danger.

ACTUARIAL ASSESSMENT OF RISK

The history of actuarial assessments of risk goes back to the 1920s, when some scholars pioneered the use of statistical predictions of recidivism and parole decisions (Borden 1924; Burgess 1928; Glueck and Glueck 1930; Hart 1923). Burgess, in one of the first sociological studies of recidivism employing statistical techniques, calculated the success rate of a sample of about three thousand parolees in the Illinois state penitentiary system (Burgess 1927). Deploying relatively simple procedures of calculation, he constructed a list of twenty-one independent variables, including factors such as age, nature of the crime, length of sentence, nationality of father, county of indictment, size of community, type of residence, and so forth. Without weighing them according to relative importance, he calculated the independent effects of these factors affecting the success or failure of parole decision based on recidivism rates. However, psychiatrists who privileged clinical judgments over the statistical procedures dominated the criminal justice system in this era. While there was a wide degree of procedural variation in clinical diagnosis of dangerousness, generally these centered on individual interviews and a series of psychological tests, as well as examination of the life history and legal records of the person under examination.

The first rumbles of discontent with clinical methods among psychiatrists emerged in the 1950s in the works of Paul E. Meehl (Grove 2005). Meehl took up the arguments made by Lundberg (1926, 1941) and Sarbin (1944) about the necessity of integrating statistical procedures in clinical predictions. Lundberg had claimed that most accurate clinical predictions were based on a methodology very similar to the ones used by statistical studies (1941, 383). Sarbin similarly had argued that those analysts who were skeptical about the statistical method and in favor of the "dynamic" clinical method were either making statistical predictions in an informal and subjective way or making completely unscientific and unreliable assertions, since all individualized judgments are affected by the psychiatric categories built on the experience of a multitude of cases (1944, 214). However, Meehl expressed doubt about the wisdom of integrating actuarial and clinical procedures, as he saw these to be fundamentally different modes of scientific analysis with the former having a better success rate in the business of making behavioral predictions (Meehl 1954).

Early experiments in the actuarial method in the post-*Baxstrom* era devised predictive instruments with relatively smaller number of variables (Monahan 1978; Monahan and Steadman 1996; Slobogin 1984). In one of the first statistical predictive studies of violent behavior, Wenk and his associates created an instrument comprised of variables such as nature of the present offense, the number of prior offenses, length of imprisonment before release, and drug use in a series of studies undertaken in the California Department of Corrections (Wenk, Robison, and Smith 1972). In their follow-up study of the *Baxstrom* patients, Steadman and Coccoza, two of the leading critics of psychiatric assessment in the criminal justice system, devised an instrument called the legal dangerousness scale. This was composed of four sets of variables: presence of juvenile record, number of previous arrests, presence of convictions for violent crimes, and severity of the crime that resulted in the present confinement (Steadman and Coccoza 1974). While these early instruments provided an alternative conceptualization of the risk of recidivism, these did not prove to be significantly more successful than traditional psychiatric assessment of dangerousness (Monahan 1978; Slobogin 1984).

A series of so-called third generation actuarial risk assessment instruments started emerging in the 1990s. One of the first of these was the result of the efforts of the MacArthur Violence Risk Assessment Study group, which began under the auspices of the National Institute of Justice and MacArthur Foundation, and it included John Monahan and Henry Steadman, both of whom were long-term critics of the clinical methods of danger assessment. The project was designed with the shortcomings of the existing risk assessment instruments in mind, including the narrow range of static predictors and a limited group of subjects, as well as the conceptual weaknesses of the explanatory variables and the fragmented nature of the past studies. The study identified a whole set of predictors including demographic, biographical, contextual, and clinical variables (Monahan et al. 2001). Most actuarial risk assessment instruments follow similar protocols of assessing the interaction between a set of individual and social variables in calculating statistical probability of violent offenses (Harris et al. 1993; Webster et al. 1995).

A hallmark of clinical analysis was the highly individualized way of analysis undertaken by each analyst, and therefore it made the appraisal of danger dependent on the perceptions and intuitions of the psychiatric professional. By contrast, actuarial instruments are designed to measure the relationship between a series of variables using statistical calculations. This very characteristic of actuarial instruments gave the impression of scientific objectivity, as it relied on concrete, quantifiable data in the analysis, and the very processes of calculation were seen as more scientific, as it allowed for replication and verification. Actuarial instruments are marked by their reliance on standardized practices, as opposed to "subjective" judgments of individual practitioners (Grove and Meehl 1996).

While there are important differences between the clinical and actuarial methods on both methodological and conceptual grounds, the boundary between the two is not as clear-cut. Some claim that intuition and subjective assessment may have their places in clinical judgment, but that does not detract from the fact that clinical practitioners mostly followed standard and structured protocols of analysis and did not arrive at conclusions in a haphazard or arbitrary way (Litwak 2001). At the same time, some of the most prevalent actuarial risk assessment instruments include parameters of analysis that are derived from clinical psychiatry. The MacArthur Violence Risk Assessment Study group has constructed a "classification tree" assessment method that combines actuarial and clinical tools (Monahan et al. 2000; Steadman et al. 2000). The Psychopathy Checklist—Revised (PCL-R) developed by Robert Hare has emerged as a widely used threat assessment instrument (Hare 1991). The PCL-R consists of statistical measures of conditions seen as predictive of psychopathic nature of an individual. Several other recent actuarial instruments, including the Violent Risk Assessment Guide (VRAG) and Historical, Clinical, Risk Management-20 (HCR-20), have adopted the basic model of PCL-R and its clinical components in their methodology of risk assessment (Harris et al. 1993; Webster et al. 1995).[1]

CRIME CONTROL AND THE RISK SOCIETY

The advances in actuarial risk assessment measures occurred in the backdrop of a political climate very conducive to penal policies that were less concerned with rehabilitation as it was with deterrence and incapacitation. James Q. Wilson has claimed that during the fall in crime rate in the mid- to late 1990s resulted partly from demographic changes, including the ageing of the Baby Boomer generation and the consequent decrease in the relative proportion of young male adults who are generally overrepresented in the ranks of offenders compared to all other demographic groups. The other, perhaps more important, reason was the strengthening of judicial, penal, and other law-enforcement measures that led to an explosion in the prison population in the 1980s, compared to the less authoritarian policies that characterized the 1960s and 1970s. Wilson adds that most violent crimes are committed by a small percentage of predatory criminals who often share a number of social and psychological characteristics—including unhealthy family environment, history of substance abuse, low verbal IQ, and emotional and temperamental deficiencies (Wilson 1995).

In identifying the most dangerous threat to public safety, Wilson argues for the need of a proactive crime control policy that would deter the risk of violent offenses through vigorous law enforcement measures. However, as some of these individuals are beyond rehabilitation and therapeutic intervention, the idea of selective incapacitation of this particularly risky group of offenders identified by actuarial methods have gained a significant amount of currency in policy circles over the last few decades. A 1982 study conducted under the auspices of the Rand Corporation used actuarial simulations of robbery cases in California, and asserted that selective incapacitation of offenders would decrease the number of offenses. It also claimed that this would allow for better allocation of government resources by putting more emphasis on high-risk offenders compared to offenders less likely to be recidivists (Greenwood and Abrahamse 1982).[2]

The conception of "actuarial justice" has generated a significant amount of scholarly interest in contemporary criminology. In their seminal works on the broader implication of the ascendency of risk management techniques, Feeley and Simon have identified a major transformation of the objectives of the criminal justice system since the 1980s. The current prevalence of risk management strategies in the criminal justice system partly grew out of a growing disillusionment with conventional law enforcement practices at the face of spiraling crime rate from the early 1970s. The historic increase in the rate of crime rate since the late 1960s, and, perhaps more importantly, rising fear of being victimized by violent and predatory offenders among people, provided a strong impetus for enacting and enforcing more stringent crime control measures. These new policies targeted certain demographic groups seen as especially prone to criminal behavior (Feeley and Simon 1994, 192). The so-called urban underclass was perceived as a special risk category, as these individuals were permanently excluded or marginalized from the economy and therefore not easily affected by rational incentives or regular strategies of deterrence.

One of the central technologies at the heart of the ideology of "new penology" is the practice of "actuarial justice." Defined as the calculability of danger through actuarial practices in decision-making in the criminal justice system, actuarial justice relies on statistical analysis of aggregate data for surveillance of populations and determination of likelihood of crime and likely offenders (Feeley and Simon 1994). Actuarial justice adapts a predominantly managerial model of crime control and is directed at efficiently managing the dangers of crime, rather than understanding the causation of crime or reform of offenders (Feeley and Simon 1992; Garland 1996). Similarly, some scholars argue that actuarial justice illustrates the broader transformation of the society and economy and the rollback of the welfare state (Garland 1996). At the heart of "the new regulatory state," according to Braithwaite, is the logic of risk-management strategies that strongly impact the criminal justice system as well as other spheres of social life (Braithwaite 2000, 228).

Unlike much of the criminological or psychopathological discourse on crime, actuarial tools are less concerned with ascertaining the social or psychological bases of criminality than they are with simply creating indices or risk factors for certain kinds of offenses. This way, these are value-neutral and objective predictive instruments that do not inquire about the larger social forces that breed crime, and simply identify certain variables related with criminality. Indeed, some have argued that a significant advantage of actuarial methods is that they identify and calculate statistical relationships between disparate variables without necessarily explaining their existence (Silver et al. 2000). This gave rise to a new approach to law enforcement and correctional practices based on managing the risk posed by individuals perceived as criminal threats as constructed by the logics of actuarial risk assessment. Thus the actuarial logic facilitates the transition from a rehabilitative model to a managerial model of crime control that accepts the inevitability of crime and attempts to prevent or manage the fallouts of crime rather than solve the problem altogether.

Feeley and Simon call the origins of actuarial reason "pre-political," that is, not easily classified by contemporary political labels. However, the widespread use of these is a fundamentally political project arising concurrently with the neoconservative social policies in the 1980s and 1990s, when the slogan of being tough on crime emerged as a *sine qua non* for political success along with attacks on big government and the welfare state. In the face of the increasing crime, drug use, and perceptions of growing incivility and fear among the citizens, there was an urgent need for the reassurance of security, and controlling the spiraling crime rate through the exercise of state power. Consequently there emerged a new form of punitiveness as a response to the problem of crime. Since the early 1980s, the political need of appearing to be "tough on crime" necessitated a public embracing of strict and punitive crime control measures, including the introduction of mandatory sentencing guidelines, reinstating the death penalty, and public stigmatization of sex offenders (Simon 1998). The reigning ideology of crime control latched on to the platform of providing public safety through imposition of severe penalties on predatory criminals. O'Malley calls it "anti-correctional" penal politics, hostile to ideals of rehabilitation or therapeutic justice (2002, 208).

Some risk researchers have argued that it is a stretch to suggest that actuarial practices are simple instruments of social power that allow the law enforcement apparatuses of the state to conduct surveillance or justify incarceration of certain sections of the population. Rather, actuarial instruments are devised to ascertain the probability of violence among individuals through scientifically tested and valid means of analysis (Webster 1998). The point, however, is not to indict scientific workers as agents of domination. Rather, the point is to note the elective affinities between the discourses of science and that of governance, and be cognizant of the ways their paths are intertwined.

The current salience of risk assessment is a recent episode in a long process of rationalization of the criminal justice system where scientific knowledge has been deployed for more efficient enforcement of law. The operational ethos of "actuarial justice" draws from assumptions and techniques that have been around for a long time. However, these are reconfigured into a new system of managing the criminal justice system. It has constructed new targets, invented new technologies of surveillance and control, and in the process led a transformation of the administration of law enforcement, judicial, and penal institutions. In our time, statistical categories have become instrumental in defining and creating new groups of offenders, and actuarial classification has become deeply ingrained in the administration of correctional measures (Feeley and Simon 1992).

At the same time, it is essential not to overstate the prevalence of actuarial methods of assessing and managing the risk of crime. Indeed, there has been a dramatic increase in the prison population in the United States, and the ideology of selective incapacitation has become increasingly prominent as a goal of penal policies. However, as recent research has shown, there are important cross-national variations in the adoption of policies of actuarial justice (O'Malley 2002). In some cases, actuarial instruments may not be necessarily utilized with the goal of selective incapacitation of violent offenders.[3] Rather, actuarial methods may be deployed to classify prisoners according for the sake of better employment of rehabilitative measures according to the needs of different segments of the prison population (Maurutto and Hannah-Moffat 2006). Indeed, actuarial instruments are part of a complex of different techniques in the administration of the criminal justice system. These may be deployed simultaneously with clinical methods of threat assessment and harm-minimization strategies, as well as technologies of therapeutic intervention (O'Malley 2004).

It is also important to note that the actuarial instruments of risk assessment are based on concepts and procedures of clinical methods that have been around for a long time. The substantive basis of Psychopathy Checklist—Revised (PCL-R), which has emerged as one of the most prominent of all actuarial tools, is rooted in the discourse of clinical psychiatry. A number of other risk assessment instruments are inspired by clinical methods, and some directly draw from the conception of psychopathology devised by Cleckley in the 1940s (Hare 1996). At the same time, the fundamental difference between clinical and actuarial threat assessment is about the very scientific conception of the criminal subject. Clinical psychiatry mostly conceptualized criminality as a binary concept—between "abnormal" and "normal" offenders—and criminal responsibility as well as criminal threat was located within the individual psyche. When it comes to the actuarial methods, however, the analytical target is not necessarily an individual who is either diagnosed as sane or insane, psychopathic, or normal. Rather, it focuses on certain behavioral indices, and calculates the probability of committing an offense among a given population. These are based on the conception of a *base rate*, or the percentage of people in a group who are likely to commit an offense under certain circumstances within a certain time span (Monahan 1981).

Thus, the language of diagnostic certainty gives way to the language of statistical probability (Reichman 1986). Guilt is presumed on the basis of actuarial tables and analytical statistics rather than legal argumentations and judicial deliberations. Assessment of criminal danger of the past centered on possibilities of rehabilitation and transformation, and consequently on individualized assessment and penal-therapeutic prescriptions. Most risk assessment measures of the present have adopted a more standardized model, in which the objective of assessment is simply identification of possible threats whose penal incapacitation needs to be tailored to the amount of danger that they pose to public safety. In sum, the subject of risk is transformed from an actual person with specific psychosocial propensities to a unit within a sample possessing certain behavioral, demographic, and social characteristics that have been shown to portend deviant tendencies by past research.

NOTES

1. However, some psychiatrists have questioned the centrality of the criminality in the clinical construct of psychopathy (Skeem and Cooke 2010).
2. Greenwood later stated that these estimates were overly optimistic (Greenwood and Turner 1987).
3. Not all recent risk assessment measures eschew the goal of rehabilitation. Indeed, risk assessment instruments such as Level of Service Inventory—Revised (LSI-R) use actuarial measures of danger along with other procedures to devise rehabilitative strategies (Hannah-Moffat 2005).

FIVE

Policing of Political Dissent

So far, the discussion has exclusively focused on the monitoring and control of the threat of crime. However, control of political dissent has been intrinsic to the governance of liberal democratic societies, and a comprehensive discussion of risk control as a governmental strategy involves the analysis of the processes of construction and surveillance of political threats. Indeed, historical experience shows that the control of radical political actors and organizations has been a special priority for law enforcement and internal security agencies as these are seen to be direct threats to the survival of the social order. Consequently, periodic campaigns of intimidation and public disinformation, as well as other legal and extralegal measures of suppression of political opposition, have been endemic in the history of American law enforcement.

THREAT OF SEDITION AND RADICALISM IN THE NINETEENTH CENTURY

The history of legislation directed at controlling political agitation and sedition goes back to the time of America's foundation. The Federalists in the Congress enacted a series of laws known as the Alien and Sedition Acts of 1798 against the backdrop of the Franco-American "pseudo-war" at the turn of the nineteenth century (Levy 1960). The "Act Concerning Aliens" (Sess. 2, Ch. 58, 1 Stat. 570) authorized the executive branch to detain and deport any noncitizen deemed dangerous to the peace and safety of the United States or suspected to be involved in any conspiracy inimical to American interests. A corollary piece of legislation, "An Act Respecting Alien Enemies" (Sess. 2, Ch. 66, 1 Stat. 577), authorized the president to order the arrest and deportation of citizens of enemy nations.

The Sedition Act formed the third pillar of the new Federalist program of domestic security in criminalizing speech, or what it saw as sedition in the form of "false, scandalous and malicious" propaganda against the government. Though war was never formally declared between France and the United States, the Alien Act and the Sedition Act became the primary weapons to suppress domestic dissent (Chaffee 1964).

The passage of these legislations occurred in a general climate of partisan politics and suspicion of widespread political conspiracy and subversion. While the threat of war subsided with the signing of the peace treaty with England, the fear of political conspiracy and insurgency was very much in the minds of some within the government. George Washington's denunciation of the Whiskey Rebellion as being influenced by secret societies of radical democratic organizations testifies to this sense of internal siege (Smelser 1954). Thus, these laws were seen as essential for the maintenance of order from the security threat posed by insufficiently patriotic citizens aided by external enemies. The Federalists, led by John Adams, were deeply suspicious of the Jeffersonian Republicans for their perceived sympathy for the revolutionaries in France. Thus the criticism of the government by some of the contemporary newspapers (sometimes edited by foreign-born citizens) was not seen as healthy debate, but as symptoms of widespread political dissent and an existential danger to the young republic. The Bill of Rights and these legislations thus represented the Janus face of democratic governance—one enshrining the inherently optimistic belief in liberty and good sense of the citizens, and the other marked by paranoia and suspicion that may not be entirely unfamiliar to people of the post–September 11 world.

While most analyses of the Sedition Act have focused on its role in curtailing free speech rights, Section 1 of the sedition legislation was solely concerned with controlling conspiracies and efforts to hinder the operations of federal laws. These legislations did not formally define what constitutes danger to public safety or sedition. Thus the interpretation of hostile conspiracy was open to interpretation and these legislations were the first in the history of the nation to provide legal justification toward establishing guilt by suspicion and by association without any recourse to due process. President Adams later claimed that there was not a single instance of actual application of the law. However, historical scholarship shows that there were several instances where government officials did attempt to use the legislation against foreigners. Additionally, the very existence of these legislations had a chilling effect on the political atmosphere and led to the voluntary departure of some individuals unwilling to run afoul of American laws (Smith 1954). The legal restrictions on free speech established by the Sedition Act in the name of maintaining popular trust in the government were complemented by the more insidious goal of surveillance and control of the political activities within the nation as established by the Alien Friends and Alien Enemies laws. Regardless of their actual extent, these legislations established the legislative and judicial precedents for the subsequent history of policing of political dissent. The fear of foreign agitators and subversives, as well as the need for effective legal (and sometimes extralegal) mechanisms of control, germinated during this period.

The growing tides of industrialization since the end of the Civil War brought with it new political threats from the Ku Klux Klan on the right, and the labor organizations on the left. The history of American labor relations in the late nineteenth century has been characterized as one of the bloodiest among all industrialized nations (Hofstader and Wallace 1971). Most companies enlisted private security and detective agencies that often responded with lethal force to organizing efforts and work actions (Norwood 2001; Smith 2003). The first generation of labor organizers faced a hostile political climate as the sympathy of the courts and governments lay overwhelmingly with business interests, and labor activists and organizations were often portrayed as radical conspiracies of socialists and anarchists.

The private security operatives employed by the corporations were not regulated or reined in by governmental supervision. Indeed, in some cases, they operated with the tacit support or active aid of government agencies. Local and state governments allowed deputizing of these operatives, which allowed them to act as officers of the law (Lens 2009). The Pinkerton National Detective Agency, established in 1850 by Alan Pinkerton, supplied trained detectives and security personnel to the corporations (Horan 1967). Pinkerton agents and company police operatives routinely infiltrated local unions to monitor and subvert organization drives (Friedman 1907). The role of the Pinkerton agency is an early chapter in the long and often murky history of collaboration between government and corporations that has come to define the economics and politics of national security in our times.[1]

In the early nineteenth century, the corporate and government attacks on labor organizations were upheld by a series of judicial decisions. The judgment on *Commonwealth v. Pullis* (1804) in Philadelphia declared labor unions to be illegal conspiracies, and consequently criminalized labor organizations that were considered a threat to democracy (Tomlins 1993). The landmark decision of the Massachusetts Supreme Court in *Commonwealth v. Hunt* (1842) recognized the legal right of workers to organize and strike (Orren 1991). However, with the intensifying of trade union activity at the end of the nineteenth century, especially the Haymarket massacre and the Pullman Strike, the conspiracy injunction was revived as a weapon against labor organizations with the active support of state legislatures and judiciaries. The judicial decisions often labeled union activities as criminal conspiracies. The Sherman Anti-Trust Law, which was originally intended to regulate corporations, was effectively turned into a weapon against the interests of organized labor by portraying unions as cartels that hindered free competition in the market.[2] Even the U.S. Supreme Court, in a series of decisions, including the famous *Re Debs* decision against Eugene Debs following the Pullman Strike, effectively criminalized work actions by unions (Goldstein 1978; Papke 1999). Similarly, in *Loewe v. Lawler* (1908) the Supreme Court ruled that Martin Lawler, a business agent of the United Hatters Union of North America, had acted illegally in organizing a boycott of the Danbury Hatters to force recognition of the union in the factory (Emery 1912; Gregory 1943).

Labor unrest was a public order problem in most industrial cities and the mining regions of the nation, albeit one in which the sympathies of the local government lay almost completely with corporate interests. The "specter of Communism" was not just haunting Europe, but also emerging as a serious threat in the minds of many political and corporate officials in the United States. The eruption of labor protest in contemporary Europe, and the events of the Paris Commune were seen as symptoms of a larger disease that would ravage the industrial order of the nation if allowed to cross the Atlantic. The labor militancy exemplified by the Molly Maguire affair and the railroad strike of 1877 represented the volatility of contemporary radicalism and the threat of an anarchist/socialist/Communist plot.[3]

The formation of the International Knights of Labor and increasing labor militancy that culminated in the Haymarket massacre were seen by many as parts of a larger radical plot of political rebellion by many in the governing circles (Goldstein 1978). The International Working People's Association, an anarchist splinter group of the Socialist Labor Party, advocated for the abolishing of the wage-labor system and adoption of militant tactics in labor organization (Foner 1975). The American Railway Union, under the leadership of Eugene Debs, called for a boycott in support of the striking Pullman workers in 1894. President Grover Cleveland called in federal troops to ensure the safety of the railroads, and Debs was arrested for criminal conspiracy (Stromquist 1987). By the end of the nineteenth century union activities only intensified and spread across the nation, bringing about even stronger response by government agencies and corporations.

The murder of Frank Little, the Industrial Workers of the World (IWW) organizer in Butte, Montana, and of countless IWW members in Everett, Washington, and the mass attack on striking copper miners in Bisbee, Arizona, testify to the violence that marked labor politics of the day. One of the most traumatic events in the history of the American labor movement occurred in April 1914, when Governor Elias Ammons called in the Colorado National Guard to control the eruption of violence during a strike called by the United Mine Workers of America in Ludlow, Colorado. In a battle with the striking miners, the National Guard unit, along with mine security officials, killed twenty-one people, including women and children (Adams 1966; Foner 1980; Gitelman 1988). The Ludlow massacre is still remembered for the sheer brutality of the events, but it was one among many cases of organized violence against workers and labor organizers in that era.

The first decades of the twentieth century only intensified political turmoil and the threat of internal subversion. The assassination of President William McKinley by Leon Czolgosz led to mass arrests of people suspected of being anarchists across the industrial areas of New York and Pennsylvania (Fine 1955). The Immigration Act of 1903, also known as the Anarchist Exclusion Act, barred anarchists, along with beggars, epileptics, and procurers of prostitutes, from entering the country (Preston 1966). The law specifically defined politically undesirable aliens as those who advocate the forceful overthrow of organized forms of government. This law was the first of a series of laws passed in this period to control the political activities of immigrants since the Alien and Seditions Acts. The suspicion of foreigners and radicals often went hand in hand, since many of the workers and union members were immigrants. The labeling of immigrants and foreigners as a potential political threat seems to have permeated the legal tradition of the nation in the twentieth century, only to be strengthened by the PATRIOT Act in our time.

FEDERALIZATION OF POLITICAL POLICING, 1918–1940

The legal persecution of labor leaders and other undesirable radical political figures reached a new height with America's entry in World War I. The newly passed Espionage Act (1917) and the Sedition Act (1918) provided law enforcement agencies with the legal muscle needed to wage a frontal assault on the more radical of trade unionists and activists many of whom were vocal against the war. Along with spying and possession of documents compromising national security, and interference with military operations, the Espionage Act also prohibited conspiracies detrimental to national security (Chafee 1919). This made it possible to widen the net to include vocal opponents of the war effort. In *Schenck v. United States*, the Supreme Court ruled that the Espionage Act did not violate free speech rights guaranteed by the First Amendment and upheld the conviction of Charles Schenck, the secretary of the Socialist Party, for agitating against the draft. In this decision, Justice Oliver Wendell Holmes established the "clear and present danger" clause that asserted that threats to collective security necessitated curbs on free speech (Kessler 1993). This opinion immortalized the phrase "shouting fire in a crowded theater," as Holmes used it to describe the possible dangers of unrestrained freedom of speech (Zinn 1980).[4]

The Sedition Act of 1918 was passed as a series of amendments to the Espionage Act in order to strengthen the provisions barring seditious speech—that is, overt opposition to the war effort (Stone 2004). This way, these amendments amounted to a reiteration of the original Alien and Sedition Acts a hundred and twenty years after the passage of the latter (Carroll 1920). However, the punishment for individuals convicted under the law was a sentence of ten to twenty years—far more than in the past. The U.S. Supreme Court upheld the law in *Abrams v. United States*. Writing for the majority, Justice John Hessin Clarke asserted that in calling for a strike in the armaments industries to protest the U.S. involvement in Russia, the defendant was guilty of sedition on the clause of "bad tendency" or the potential to incite illegal and radical actions. Justice Holmes, along with Justice Louis Brandeis, dissented in this case, as they did not see any "clear or present danger" to the government and the nation related to the defendant's action (Chafee 1919).

In 1918, federal marshals, along with local law enforcement agencies, raided the headquarters of the IWW in Chicago, and in other offices across the nation. The top leaders of the IWW were arrested in one sweep. After almost eight months of detention, they were put on trial for conspiracy. Eugene Debs was himself arrested for resisting the draft, and sentenced to ten years in prison and stripped of citizenship. In *Debs v. United States*, the Supreme Court upheld the conviction on grounds essentially the same as the Schenck case. The end of the war rendered the Espionage and the Sedition Acts superfluous, and Congress repealed the laws in 1921 (Hagedorn 2007). Debs was pardoned by President Warren Harding, and freed from prison in the same year.

Existing criminal statutes in the states were often used against political activists. Several members of the Communist Labor Party of California were arrested and convicted on the basis of the 1919 Criminal Syndicalism Act in the state that defined advocacy and incitement of unlawful acts of force as a criminal felony. In its ruling on *Whitney v. California* (1927), resulting from an appeal by one of the defendants, Anita Whitney, the Supreme Court unanimously decided that the state government did not violate the Fourteenth Amendment, since it had the right to detain or punish anyone who abused the right of free speech by inciting disobedience to the government and inciting violence.[5] Justice Brandeis concurred with the court on procedural grounds, but wrote an impassioned plea in defense of freedom of speech (Blasi 1988; Strum 1993):

> Fear of serious injury cannot alone justify suppression of free speech and assembly. Men feared witches and burnt women. It is the function of speech to free men from the bondage of irrational fears. To justify suppression of free speech there must be reasonable ground to fear that serious evil will result if free speech is practiced. There must be reasonable ground to believe that the danger apprehended is imminent. There must be reasonable ground to believe that the evil to be prevented is a serious one. . . . Those who won our independence by revolution were not cowards. They did not fear political change. They did not exalt order at the cost of liberty. To courageous, self-reliant men, with confidence in the power of free and fearless reasoning

> applied through the processes of popular government, no danger flowing from speech can be deemed clear and present, unless the incidence of the evil apprehended is so imminent that it may befall before there is opportunity for full discussion. (Brandeis 1927)[6]

The direct involvement of the federal security agencies in monitoring and controlling the threat of political subversion began after World War I (Feurlicht 1971; Hoyt 1969; Kaross 1989). In a climate of fear of subversion and rebellion in the face of widespread labor unrest in the nation and the Bolshevik revolution in Russia, many in the U.S. government were convinced of revolutionary plots by radical elements within the nation (Hagedorn 2007).[7] Contemporary Attorney General A. Michael Palmer established the General Intelligence Division (GID) within the Bureau of Investigation of the Justice Department under the leadership of J. Edgar Hoover (Coben 1963). The Bureau of Investigation agents, under the leadership of Palmer, arrested scores of immigrant workers and union activists in a sweep later known as the infamous "Palmer Raids." Many of these individuals were deported as the Immigration Act (1918) construed political radicalism as a ground for denying citizenship.[8]

The contemporary assistant secretary of labor, Louis Freeland Post, was a firm opponent of the raids and detention of immigrants on charges of radicalism. He granted hearings to the people charged of sedition by the Bureau of Investigation, and dismissed a number of deportation cases against immigrant labor organizers (Post 1923). This earned Post the enmity of the Bureau of Investigation and a number of others in the U.S. Congress, who called for his impeachment. However, Post successfully defended himself in a hearing before the Congress, and continued on in his position until his retirement in 1923. Over three thousand people were arrested over a period of six months, many of them on rather dubious grounds. The raids and the arrests ceased after a decision by the U.S. District Court of Massachusetts declared them as illegal and freed seventeen of the detainees (Murray 1955).

The Palmer Raids firmly established the tradition of policing of political threats by the federal agencies. The Bureau of Investigation under William J. Burns during the Harding administration conducted wiretapping and secret surveillance of politicians and newspaper editors critical of extrajudicial authority of the government. The GID compiled a dossier on thousands of suspected radicals in this period (Fox 2004). Attorney General Harlan Fiske Stone ousted Burns, and appointed Hoover in his place in 1924. Hoover was given explicit orders to cease and desist from all domestic political surveillance programs, and the works of the GID was suspended for over a decade until the newly formed Federal Bureau of Investigation (FBI) revived it in the 1930s (Goldstein 1978; Williams 1981).

THE LONG SHADOW OF MCCARTHY: POLICING OF RADICALISM IN THE MID-CENTURY

In the mid-1930s, Hoover, as the director of the newly established Federal Bureau of Investigation, was asked by President Franklin Delano Roosevelt to establish a program of monitoring and disrupting political subversion by suspected Communist and Fascist agents and sympathizers within the nation. As the FBI was prohibited from conducting political surveillance, a legal loophole was used, whereas the FBI could conduct investigations about "general intelligence" matters if asked to do so by the State Department in the name of national security (Andrew 1995; Donner 1980). Hoover revived the GID, which prepared a Security Index, or a list of individuals deemed to be security threats (Theoharis 1978a). As World War II started in Europe, the responsibility of counterespionage and investigation of subversive activities was delegated to the FBI, along with the Office of Naval Intelligence and Military Intelligence Department, by a presidential emergency order (Donner 1980). The Security Index was complemented with a custodial detention index of individuals with Fascist or Communist affiliations or sympathies, and the FBI prepared a contingency plan to detain them in the case of a national emergency (Theoharis 1978b).

The detention plan was maintained through the 1940s. Newly declassified documents show that with the outbreak of hostilities in Korea, Hoover sought permission from President Harry Truman to suspend the writ of habeas corpus and arrest around twelve thousand suspected "disloyal" citizens (*Washington Post* 2007). While this may seem as somewhat Orwellian in retrospect, it is essential to remember that the internment of Japanese Americans during World War II had already set judicial and operational precedents for mass arrests and incarcerations with little oversight or accountability. The history of national emergencies (or mere threats thereof) shows the extraordinary demonstrations of sovereign power in democratic societies—often with active, or at least passive, acquiescence of the citizenry.

New legislative and administrative maneuvers bolstered the mechanisms of surveillance and control of "subversive" and "seditious" elements within the nation began even before the actual entry of the United States in World War II. The U.S. House of Representatives established the House Committee on Un-American Activities (HCUA) in 1937 to investigate Nazi sympathizers and members of the Ku Klux Klan. However, the focus of attention soon shifted to the threat of Communism (Goodman 1968). The Hatch Act of 1939 ("An Act to Prevent Pernicious Political Activities") forbade federal employees to be involved in political activities, especially as members of political groups that advocated the overthrow of the constitutional government. The Alien Registration Act, or the Smith Act, was enacted in 1940 (Mansfield 1941). The actual import of the law far exceeded the stated goal of registration of noncitizens. It simultaneously sought to control and punish seditious and subversive actions. Thus, it prohibited the advocacy or propagation of radical politics and membership in subversive political groups. Indeed, the first major criminal case resulting from the law was the trial of the leadership of the Socialist Worker's Party in Minneapolis on grounds of political subversion and the propagation of Trotskyite ideas. The jury found twelve defendants, out of the twenty-three people charged for the crime, guilty of circulating radical literature and consequently of advocating the overthrow of the government (Stone 2004). The Communist Party of the United States (CPUS) initially supported the trial, given the split between Stalin and Trotsky. However, the leadership of the Communist Party was put on trial on the basis of the Smith Act in 1949, and all eleven defendants received prison sentences of varying lengths. The Supreme Court upheld the convictions in *Dennis v. United States,* when it ruled that the conviction of Eugene Dennis, the general secretary of the CPUS, did not violate the First Amendment (Wiecek 2001).

By the time the Korean War started, the second "Red Scare" was already well under way. This period saw a number of efforts in the U.S. Congress (and some state legislatures) to establish a system requiring formal registration of Communist activists in order to facilitate monitoring and control of their political activities (Hunt 1955). Representatives Karl Mundt of South Dakota and Richard Nixon of California introduced the Mundt-Nixon Bill that required the registration of Communists and barred them from holding public office (Chafee 1950). The bill passed in the House of Representatives in 1948. Much of the spirit of the Mundt-Nixon bill and other subsequent bills introduced by Representative Mundt along with Representatives Ferguson and Johnston was assimilated in the Internal Security Act of 1950 (ISA), introduced by Senator Patrick McCarran of Nevada (Kirshen 1951). The McCarran Act authorized the investigation of suspected Communist activists, registration of Communist-affiliated organizations, and the detention of "dangerous" individuals in the events of war or domestic insurrection (Griffith 1971). Title I of the McCarran Act established a new federal committee responsible for the investigation of suspected Communist organizations and affiliated organizations, called the Subversive Activities Control Board. Title II of the McCarran Act, or the Emergency Detention Act, sought to detain any person suspected of radical political activities and consequently posing a danger to the elected government of the United States.[9] Congress appropriated funds to be used to maintain detention camps within the nation for this purpose (Cotter and Smith 1957).

President Truman vetoed the legislation on grounds of its infringement of civil liberties—indeed, he called it the greatest threat to civil liberties since the Alien and Sedition Acts. At the same time, President

Truman's impeccable credentials in fighting Communism abroad matched some of his domestic policies as well and he showed little patience with subversive or radical politics. He initiated a loyalty program for federal employees by Executive Order 9835, which mandated the dismissal of individuals on the basis of reasonable suspicion of disloyalty. He also instructed the attorney general to investigate individuals with questionable political ideals by establishing a Loyalty Review Board for federal employees (Kemper 1965). The McCarran Act was one of many anti-Communist laws in the heyday of Senator Joseph McCarthy and the HCUA. The Communist Control Act of 1954, signed into effect by President Eisenhower, outlawed the Communist Party of the United States and criminalized Communist affiliations. However, the law granted Fifth Amendment protection to individuals under investigation.

At the height of the McCarthy era, a series of decisions by the Supreme Court under Chief Justice Earl Warren challenged the constitutionality of some of the aspects of the legal suppression of Communism. The conflict between free speech guaranteed by the First Amendment and the criminalization of the espousal of radical politics by the Smith Act constituted the basis of *Yates v. United States* (1957). Fourteen leaders of the Communist Party in California were convicted in the charge of advocacy of forceful overthrow of the U.S. government. In a certiorari issued to the U.S. Court of Appeals for the Ninth Circuit, the Supreme Court opined, in a six-to-one decision, that there is a difference between political advocacy at an abstract level and concrete actions of inciting violence and overthrow of the government. Thus the First Amendment protects political speech unless there is "clear and present danger" of mass rebellion (Linde 1970).

However, the registration clause of the McCarran Act was upheld by the Supreme Court in its decision on *Communist Party of the United States v. Subversive Activities Control Board* (1961), with the dissent of four justices, including Chief Justice Earl Warren. However, the decision was overturned four years later, when the Supreme Court ruled that the requirement of registration for Communist party members violated their Fifth Amendment rights in *Albertson v. Subversive Activities Control Board* (1965). Similarly, in *United States v. Robel* the Supreme Court again ruled in favor of the defendant who was indicted for continuing to work for a defense installment in spite of his membership in the Communist Party. Writing for the majority, Chief Justice Warren asserted, "Congress, in exercising its ample power to safeguard the national defense, cannot exceed constitutional bounds, particularly where First Amendment rights are at stake" (U.S. Supreme Court 1967). The Warren Court came under sustained criticism from members of both houses of Congress who saw the court decisions against McCarthyism as well as racial segregation as a sign of the activist turn of the Supreme Court to the liberal side of the political spectrum (Kemper 1965).

In spite of the official repudiation of McCarthyism at the end of the decade, covert operations against activists deemed to be a threat to the political status quo have been ongoing since the mid-1950s (Davis 1997). The FBI under Hoover began the secretive and the mostly illegal Counter-Intelligence Program (COINTELPRO) of domestic surveillance and counter-subversive activities in order to monitor, disrupt, and discredit political groups deemed to be a threat to the government (Davis 1992). COINTELPRO gathered strength at the wake of the civil rights movement and student radicalism in the 1960s (Cunningham 2004; Theoharis 1978a). Uncovering of secret documents listing the range of activities in the targeting of radical political groups of both left- and right-wing persuasions gives testimony to the length government security agencies could go to with the tacit approval, or at least acquiescence, of a section of elected governments in a democratic society (Blackstock 1988; Churchill and Vander Wall 2002).

The discovery of the so-called Huston Plan, a report prepared by President Nixon's aide Tom Huston in 1970 on the control of the growing tides of radicalism among the nation's youth over the past decade, came with the Watergate investigations. The Huston Plan detailed a set of proposed counter-espionage and surveillance operations including illegal surveillance of mail and telephones and warrantless searches of premises, as well as an outline of a contingency detention plan of suspected subversives and radicals (SSCSGORIA 1976). It was surprisingly opposed by J. Edgar Hoover, and was never enacted in its entirety (Theoharis 1978a). However, the break-in at Watergate, the disclosure of the White House enemies list, and other related governmental excesses during that era demonstrate the seriousness of the intention of the people behind the plan.

In 1976, the U.S. Senate convened the Select Committee to Study Governmental Operations with Respect to Intelligence Activities, under the leadership of Senator Frank Church (D-ID). The Church Committee publicly repudiated COINTELPRO and other illegal espionage and intelligence operations undertaken by governmental agencies in the 1960s and 1970s. It also made a series of recommendations regarding operational guidelines regarding domestic and international intelligence activities. The passage of the Foreign Intelligence Surveillance Act (FISA) in 1978 was directly influenced by the recommendations of the Church Committee. The FISA imposed strict limits on surveillance and intelligence operations. It established special FISA courts for judicial review of intelligence activities in the form assuming the authority of issuing warrants for surveillance requests made by governmental agencies on suspected foreign agents. In spite of considerable opposition from a section of the intelligence community and public criticism by some political figures, the recommendation of the Church Committee and the FISA guidelines regulated domestic intelligence operations in the nation until recently.

The history of suppression of political dissent and the surveillance of individuals and organizations suspected of professing radical beliefs provide numerous examples of the extraordinary lengths to which state apparatuses are willing to go in order to counter any significant threat to the political order. This history also demonstrates that in many cases people once vilified as public enemies have later been absolved by judicial decisions, and vindicated by history. When people deemed security threats are allowed public trials and legal defense, it provides a communicative space for the discussion, deliberation, and, ultimately, the assignment of guilt or declaration of innocence. But as the history of political policing in the United States shows, in a number of cases the assessment of threat takes place behind closed doors, and is decided by nameless and faceless bureaucrats without any judicial or procedural recourse. Indeed, this history shows a very strong family resemblance to what the former vice president Dick Cheney has called the necessity of going to the "dark side" in order to safeguard the democratic way of life. These lessons from the past are particularly relevant and instructive in contextualizing the campaign against terrorism in our times. The next chapter analyzes the transformation of governmental powers and security practices since September 11, 2001.

NOTES

1. During the Civil War, Pinkerton served in the intelligence service of the Union Army and was reputed to have thwarted the Baltimore plot against President Abraham Lincoln's life (Cuthbert 1949).

2. The subsequent Clayton Anti-Trust Act of 1914 exempted union activity from the purview of anti-trust regulations by arguing that human labor is not a commodity (Kovner 1947; Meltzer 1965).

3. The sensational crimes attributed to the so-called Molly Maguires, a secret society that supposedly originated in Ireland and was active in the coal mines of Pennsylvania, captivated public attention in the 1870s (Dewees 1877). The trial of the Molly Maguires had a destructive effect on labor organizations in the area (Broehl 1964). The trial rested on the testimony of a Pinkerton detective, and Arthur Conan Doyle immortalized this story in *The Valley of Fear*. Historians have questioned the links between the crimes and unions (Kenny 1998).

4. Justice Holmes's original statement read, "The most stringent protection of free speech would not protect a man *falsely* shouting fire in a theater and causing a panic" (emphasis added). The word "falsely" appears to have dropped in most usages of the phrase.

5. The decision was overturned more than forty years later by *Brandenburg v. Ohio* in 1969 (Linde 1970). The Supreme Court ruled that the advocacy of the use of force or violation of law does not constitute an offense until there is imminent danger of lawlessness resulting from such speech (Lynd 1975). Brandenburg was a local Ku Klux Klan leader—thus the principle of "clear and present danger" came a full circle from the threat of radical political of the left to the right.

6. Ms. Whitney was later pardoned by the governor of California.

7. The Posse Comitatus Act forbade operations by the U.S. military forces within the nation. However, the threat of internal and external enemies during World War I

led to involvement of army intelligence operatives within the nation in gathering intelligence about domestic and external subversives. The War Department had created the Military Intelligence Division (MID) under Colonel Ralph Henry Van Deman. Van Deman actively recruited both military and civilian agents for intelligence gathering operations within the nation. These operations were not limited to the monitoring of agents of enemy nations. Historical records show that MID was involved in the surveillance of union officials and members of the National Association for the Advancement of Colored People (NAACP) even after the signing of the armistice with Germany (Jensen 1991). Military involvement in gathering information of individuals and groups deemed as domestic political threats continued through the 1930s (Talbert 1991).

8. Perhaps the most famous incident of deportation resulting from a Palmer raid happened in December 1919, when 249 suspected radicals, including Emma Goldman, were sent to Russia on the Soviet ship *Buford.*

9. While it was the target of concerted attack by civil libertarians, and some Democratic congress members, the Detention Act remained in the books until 1971, when Public Law 92-128 codified in 18 U.S.C. § 4001(a) repealed it (Longaker 1974).

SIX

"Risk Wars": The Campaign against Terrorism

In spite of the apparent similarities with violent crime, acts of terrorism are conceptually distinctive because these are defined by political goals rather than individual motives (Barak 2004). However, criminologists are becoming more and more conscious of the possible utility of applying criminological insights in the study of terrorist violence (LaFree and Dugan 2004; Rosenfeld 2004). The label of terrorism has frequently been subject to political bias, and dispassionate analysis is often complicated, given the strong emotions associated with the toll of political terror. The imperative of managing terrorism-related risks has not only changed the organization and practices of government agencies, but also resulted in the development of a number of invasive security practices. In spite of their conspicuous authoritarianism, the security measures instituted by governmental agencies have often been met with approval or at least, resigned acceptance of people. Governing the new world of global terror has resulted in a culture of eternal vigilance and suspicion with potentially destructive consequences for liberal democracies.

LEGAL RESPONSE TO TERRORISM

The governmental response to the attacks on September 11 took the form of a series of legislative and executive measures directed at the reorganization of intelligence and security apparatuses, as well as the vast expansion of surveillance powers of the state. Perhaps the most famous example of this is the USA PATRIOT Act[1] (Public Law 107-56) that passed in the immediate aftermath of the attacks. The Patriot Act included separate provisions for reorganizing security organizations, enhancing intelligence, stopping the finances of terrorist organizations, and strengthening border security criminal laws, as well as streamlining aids and compensations to victims of terrorist attacks. Title II of the law that centered on the expansion of surveillance procedures has emerged as the most controversial aspect of the legislation. The PATRIOT Act created a new category of "enhanced surveillance procedures" that granted the FBI and other law enforcement agencies permission to conduct surveillance of both U.S. citizens and noncitizens alike and removed most of the restrictions on intelligence-gathering operations established by the FISA. It also expanded the authority of government agencies to issue the so-called National Security Letters that allow them to monitor communication and financial records of a person without a court order (Public Law 107-56, Title 5, § 505).[2] The enhanced surveillance powers included the permission for monitoring all forms of communications used by a suspected individual with an order from a judge from any district court or a U.S. Court of Appeals (Public Law 107-56, Title 2, § 216). The FBI was also allowed to delay notification of executing a warrant, effectively authorizing the entry and searching of suspected individuals' homes or workplaces without their permission or knowledge (Public Law 107-56, Title 2, § 213).[3] The PATRIOT Act also significantly strengthened the existing immigration laws. The changes made in the border security and immigration provisions have included draconian provisions regarding the reservation of authority to detain illegal immigrants or those suspected of being connected, however remotely, to terrorist activities without a hearing for extended periods of time (Title IV, Subtitle B, § 412).

The largest reorganization of the federal security institutions with the passage of the Homeland Security Act of 2002 (Public Law No. 107-296, 116 Stat. 2135) closely followed the passage of the PATRIOT Act. It established the Department of Homeland Security (DHS) that brought together twenty-two existing federal security and emergency management organizations, and established the cabinet-level post of secretary of homeland security. The formation of the DHS came with the realization for the greater need of coordination and consolidation of security practices at the federal level, and the reorganization of the security apparatuses in the post–Cold War era where the primary national threats may not come from other nation states, but rather from small groups or an individual intent on committing acts of terror.

In December 2004, the U.S. Senate passed the Intelligence Reform and Terrorism Prevention Act (Public Law 108-458) with a great amount of bipartisan support. Like the previous national security laws passed since September 11, the IRTPA sought to streamline and rationalize a wide range of intelligence, immigration, and anti-terror policies. It established the new position of director of national intelligence as the head of the intelligence community, and serves as an advisor to the National Security Council. The post was created to establish objectives, priorities, and guidelines of intelligence operations, as well as to facilitate better coordination between the various civilian and military agencies engaged in intelligence and security related operations (118 Stat. 3651). The law also established directives for the enhancement of border security through significantly increasing the allocation for technological and human resources deemed necessary for effective surveillance of the border (118 Stat. 3733). It also made significant changes to immigration matters in order to identify and deter potential threats from using the asylum and legal immigration channels to gain entry into the nation. It likewise strengthened measures to stop the flow of money to finance suspected terrorist groups (118 Stat. 3750, § 6303). It broadened the definition of aiding and abetting terrorists by inserting the definition of "material support," defined as providing any tangible or intangible support including money, shelter, training, advice, transportation, weapons and other equipment, and false identity documents (118 Stat. 3762, § 6603).

The creation of the DHS and the passage of the PATRIOT Act alarmed many because of the vast expansion of government power with potentially deleterious effects on civil liberties and privacy of citizens. However, there were still concerns among some in the government that these did not do enough to establish a comprehensive system of security against terrorism-related threats. The Department of Justice under Attorney General John Ashcroft drafted a law titled Domestic Security Enhancement Act of 2003 (Lewis and Mayle 2003). The DSEA, also called PATRIOT Act II, never actually became a law. Indeed, the draft was never even introduced to Congress. However, the major sections of the draft bill represented a massive expansion of the already-heightened power of control of the executive branch and federal security agencies without any form of judicial oversight.

The USA PATRIOT Act and Terrorism Prevention Reauthorization Act of 2005 reauthorized most of the provisions of the PATRIOT Act and the subsequent Intelligence Reform and Terrorism Prevention Act of 2004. This law also authorized certain new measures concerning the control of financing of terrorist groups and anti-drug initiatives. Additionally, the USA PATRIOT Act Additional Reauthorizing Amendments Act of 2006 revised the procedures for the issuance of National Security Letters. Section 215 of the PATRIOT Act forbade the disclosure of any demand by the FBI to check business records of an individual. The additional reauthorization law imposed a new one-year limit to the nondisclosure clause, and allowed the recipient of such orders to petition a FISA court modify or nullify such agreements. It also exempted library records of an individual from purview of National Security Letters, which was originally imposed by the PATRIOT Act.

The so-called Terrorist Surveillance Program (TSP) was initiated immediately after September 11 by a presidential directive. The TSP authorized the National Security Agency (NSA) to intercept any form of electronic or telecommunication originating from abroad without a warrant even if one of the parties to the communication was located within the United States. The fact that the NSA routinely monitors worldwide telecommunication networks should not come as a surprise to anyone familiar with the ways of the U.S. intelligence institutions. Indeed, the NSA has been running such a signals-intelligence program code-named ECHELON with collaboration with Australia, Canada, New Zealand, and the United Kingdom since the height of the Cold War. The precursor of the NSA, the Armed Forces Security Agency, initiated Project Shamrock and Project Minaret, which monitored electronic and telegraphic communications of suspected domestic subversives (SSCSGORIA 1976). However, these invasive surveillance programs were found to be in violation of the Fourth Amendment on several grounds, and the FISA (1978) was created precisely to establish some form of judicial oversight on secret intelligence programs that may affect U.S. citizens (Daily 2006). The NSA surveillance programs in the wake of September 11 were established to bypass such oversights in the name of greater effectiveness of intelligence operations against the moving targets of international terrorists and their domestic sympathizers (Gonzales 2005). In 2006, former Senator Arlen Specter (R-PA) introduced a bill titled the National Security Surveillance Act of 2006 (NSSA). The NSSA was passed by the Senate Judiciary Committee but was not passed as a law by the Senate or the House. It would have established a degree of judicial control in the form of warrants but limited the restrictions imposed by the FISA; it would also have significantly increased the powers or surveillance of the intelligence community, especially in times of national emergencies and wars (Wong 2006).

The disclosure of the warrantless surveillance program, including the monitoring of American citizens, created a furor among legislators and citizens alike. In order to provide legal cover for the surveillance program, Congress passed a set of new legislations during the waning years of the Bush administration. The Protect America Act (2007) was the first major revision of the FISA. It loosened the requirement of warrants for both domestic and foreign surveillance, and gave full authority of surveillance protocols to officers of national security field offices, but they were required to inform the FISA court within seventy-two hours (Public Law 110-155, § 105(b)). It exempted intelligence surveillance operations in foreign nations from needing warrants, and allowed for the monitoring of all communication within the nation as long as it does not specifically target a person within the country. It also removed other restrictions imposed on surveillance by the FISA by removing the requirement of designation of the target individual as a foreign agent, thereby reserving the authority to monitor any individual suspected of collaboration or association with a terrorist regardless of their nationality. The Protect America Act and the subsequent FISA Amendments Act of 2008 provided legislative cover for the continuation of broad surveillance and granted immunity to telecommunication companies complicit in surveillance programs by government agencies from lawsuits or public investigations, though there was significant opposition to this provision in the U.S. House of Representatives. The FISA was amended to grant government agencies the authority not to maintain surveillance records or destroy such records in the name of national security. It also extended the period of warrantless surveillance, and allowed to classify as secret the names and other descriptions of the subjects of surveillance. While civil libertarians expressed grave concern over the extension of the federal government's police powers, the presidential candidates of both parties, Senators Barack Obama and John McCain, extended their support for the revisions of the FISA (Kane 2008).

In 2007, Representative Jane Harman (D-CA) introduced the Violent Radicalization and Homegrown Terrorism Prevention Act (HR 1955) in the House of Representatives. The act was designed to amend the Homeland Security Act (2002) in order to deter the rise of radical politics and possible threats of terrorism from within the nation. It was specifically focused at the prevention of "violent radicalization," defined as advocacy of political extremism in order to promote ideological, political, or religious objectives, and "the use, planned use, or threatened use of force or violence by a group or individual to promote the group or individual's political, religious, or social beliefs" (HR 1955, 2007). The bill was passed in the house in October 2007, but was not passed by the Senate. Consequently, it never became a law. The bill generated a significant amount of controversy from both ends of the political spectrum, and united Representative Dennis Kucinich (D-OH) with Representatiuve Ron Paul (R-TX), and the American Civil Liberties Union with the John Birch Society. Most of the criticisms centered on the impact of the proposed law on civil liberties and the right of free speech as it would have resulted in effectively criminalizing thought and speech without any overt actions of violence. The controversy surrounding the law was reminiscent of the various interpretations of the "clear and present danger" test almost eighty years after Justice Holmes first established it.

The threat of terrorism is not just limited to the United States (Jackson and Parks 2007). Since 2001, a number of European states have enacted anti-terror legislations to control the threat of terror as well. While most of these nations have faced the threat of internal terrorism in the past, as a consequence of either ethno-nationalist struggles (the United Kingdom and Spain) or radical left-wing groups in the 1970s and 1980s (Germany and Italy), the threat of terrorism inspired by radical Islamic groups has resulted in the adoption of stringent security measures. Most of these have resulted in some controversy regarding the relative balance of civil liberties and enhanced police powers (Stevenson 2003; Tsoukala 2006).

The British Anti-terrorism, Crime and Security Act (2001) contained provisions for indefinite detention of foreigners suspected of involvement in terrorist activities (Cram 2009; Forster 2009). The expansion of police power, including the enhanced "stop and search" authority without provable grounds of reasonable suspicion, has generated controversy on grounds of civil liberty issues and the possibility of increased racial and ethnic profiling (Hallsworth 2006). The Terrorism Act of 2006, passed after the July 2005 bombings in London, criminalized incitements to terrorist action—that is, "a statement that is likely to be understood by some or all of the members of the public to whom it is published as a direct or indirect encouragement or other inducement to them to the commission, preparation or instigation of acts of terrorism or Convention offences" (British Parliament 2006, 1). Though the law called for allowing detention of terror suspects without charge for a period of ninety days, the House of Commons voted this down. Yet this legislation doubled the period of detention to four weeks from the previous fourteen days set by the Criminal Justice Act of 2003.

Controversial as it is, indefinite detention has emerged as a weapon of choice in the campaign against terrorism and violent crimes. Most other western European democracies also have used it in periodic drives against political extremism. Germany has had relatively strong anti-terror laws since the days of the Red Army Faction (RAF) in the 1970s (Boyne 2004). At the height of the political turmoil created by the arrest and trial of the leadership of the RAF, the West German government authorized the detaining and holding of political prisoners and terrorists incommunicado for prolonged periods of time. This was extended in 2006 to all criminal cases. The Spanish Criminal Prosecution Act allows holding suspects incommunicado with the permission of a judge. The Code of Criminal Procedure in France similarly allows for solitary confinement of a detainee up to a period of three months (Oehmichen 2008).

A significant number of Western European nations have a sizeable Muslim minority population often marginalized in the culture, economy, and the polity. Recent terrorist bombings in London and Madrid have exacerbated the threat perception of a radicalized group of "homegrown" terrorists. The official and popular discourse on immigration is increasingly subsumed under a wider discourse of security, and much of the debates on immigration center on policies of effective border control and surveillance (Bigo 2002; Geddes 2003; Ibrahim 2005; Karyotis 2007; Lodge 2004). Since September 11, the German government has revoked immunity for religious groups from government surveillance, and adopted other measures to monitor and control the entry and exit of immigrants suspected of terrorist association (Miko and Froehlich 2004).

Immigration policies in the member states of the European Union have undergone significant revisions in order to allow for more rigorous scanning of asylum seekers and immigrants alike, in order to be able to block individuals suspected of being a potential threat to public order or domestic security (Bicchi and Martin 2006). The European Council called for the adoption of measures for ascertaining that the asylum seeker had no links to or sympathies for terrorist groups or actions (European Council 2001). The Council also called for better intelligence, adoption of new biometric technologies, and greater communication between various intelligence and security departments of the member nations in order to be able to screen and identify those involved with terrorism.

TERRORISM AND THE "RISK SOCIETY"

The "old terrorism" of the twentieth century was mostly motivated by ethnic nationalism or far-left ideologies, and used violence as a technique to capture state power or bargain with national governments in order to achieve its goals. However, the rise of the "new terrorism" of the Al-Qaeda variety has transformed the fields of governance. The enemy in this case is a faceless, deterritorialized entity, and often organized as a loose amalgamation of autonomous cells that are not easily deterred or controlled by conventional military or law-enforcement techniques. The threat of new terrorism results in the reorganizing the practices of security by suturing together elements from doctrines of the military, espionage, law enforcement, and counter-terrorism institutions—not always in a seamless manner, as policy debates on detainees in the so-called War on Terrorism has shown in recent times.

Ulrich Beck has recently commented that the governmental response to the events of September 11 has led to a fundamental transformation in the security doctrine of liberal democracies. The consequent development of the paradigm of "risk wars" have involved armed intervention across the globe to fight supposedly hostile forces in order to preempt the threat of a terrorist attack while minimizing risk to the soldiers on the field and citizens at home (2009, 150). These entail a new logic of legitimation of armed intervention since the global war on terror declared by the Bush administration resulted in upending the traditional rules of war based on the Westphalian system of nations. A declaration of war on non-state actors requires "cosmopolitan legitimation" of a UN Security Council resolution. In lieu of that (as was the case with the war with Iraq in 2003), it is legitimized as a preemption of a global risk or a threat to the whole of humanity.

Within the domestic sphere these wars are presented as a necessary prerequisite for maintaining the security of a nation. In contrast to the total wars of the early twentieth century, where the entire nation was mobilized in the war effort, these new campaigns take place elsewhere hidden from the public eye beyond what is presented by a pliable media. Facts are carefully edited, presented, and sometimes invented in order to sell these to a fearful public as essential for their own safety. Most importantly, discussions and deliberations about risk analysis and management techniques that often used to be in the public domain are now shrouded in a cloak of secrecy, and monopolized by the professional expertise of the military, security, espionage, and counter-terrorism apparatuses of the state: "The power of definition of experts has been replaced by that of states and intelligence agencies; and the pluralisation of expert rationalities has turned into the simplification of enemy images" (Beck 2002, 45).

Despite all efforts, a complete sense of security from the threat of terrorism has been elusive. This way, the threat of new terrorism is very much in line with the travails and tribulations of the risk society before September 11. Beck has pointed out that manufactured hazards that plague the risk society are highly mobile and not contained by national boundaries or any other spatial barriers. This represents the processes of individualization and globalization of war. Wars in the past were waged between national armies, or irregular forces claiming allegiance to a nation. Terrorism of the present, however, may be seen as a war waged by an individual against a state or a community. The technologies of destruction that defined the uneasy peace though the Cold War—chemical, biological, and nuclear weapons—and were monopolized by state agencies are now sought by individuals in their pursuit of creating death and destruction in massive scale.

New terrorism is global in its nature and scope. The precise character of new terrorism defies the organizational, ideological, and locational precedents of the terrorist groups of the twentieth century. Al-Qaeda and other fellow travelers in the path of terror are loosely organized in independent and autonomous cells that greatly reduce the effectiveness of traditional security and counter-terrorist measures against this multiheaded and multimodal threat. These groups may take aim at any nation perceived to be an enemy, and may comprise of citizens who have not demonstrated any previous signs of political militancy. Effective policing of these threats is problematized by the fact that the potential offenders do not always share demographics or any other characteristics that are generally used in constructing risk indices.

The threat of terrorism since September 11 potentially mirrors the magnitude of the potential technological or environmental catastrophes that define the nature of the risk society. The threat of nuclear fallout or environmental degradation has threatened much of the advanced industrialized world over the last thirty years, or is analogous to the threat of international terrorism in this way. Some of the risks posed by technological developments are gradual and not immediately felt. However, like a nuclear disaster, the risk of terrorism is immediate and potentially just as catastrophic. Indeed, one of the threats frequently cited by governments is the relentless pursuit of a nuclear device by terrorist organizations.

Despite all the stories about "loose nukes" in the former Soviet republics, the risk of infiltration of the nuclear arsenal of Pakistan, or the nonexistent weapons of mass destruction possessed by Saddam Hussein, such weapons appear to have been elusive for terrorist groups so far. However, a device for spreading radioactive agents, or a so-called dirty bomb, still happens to be very much in the reckoning of both the terrorist and security agencies. It is not a coincidence that one of the first arrests of a homegrown Al-Qaeda operative on United States, Jose Padilla, was originally accused of conspiring to obtain and use such a device in the U.S. soil.

Beck has argued that the problem of terrorism goes beyond the purview of the traditional techniques of controlling technological or environmental risks. The insurance principle that underlined much of risk management techniques has been rendered obsolete by the "intentional risk" (Beck 2002). While terrorism-related risk does pose a challenge, empirical investigations have shown that the threat of terrorism has also reconfigured the practices of the insurance industry. Since the events of September 11, the American insurance industry has lobbied the federal government of the United States for direct support in providing insurance at the face of the threat of terrorism, and actively sought to reshape the market for catastrophic insurance (Ericson and Doyle 2004).[4] These efforts have been largely successful, and the Terrorism Risk Insurance Act, passed by the U.S. Senate in 2002, has asserted that the government should act as the insurer of the last resort for catastrophic events while mechanisms of providing insurance by private corporations are worked out in these uncertain time (Aradau and Van Munster 2007). Some European nations that have faced the threat of domestic terrorism in the past have instituted programs for making terrorism insurance available to the citizens by forming public/private partnerships between the insurance industry and the government. The British government set up the *Pool Re* program in 1993 to meet the challenges of terrorism, which has been extended since September 11 (Dorn and Levi 2006).

The reconfiguration of the governmental functions in the post–September 11 period has included private enterprises assuming a greater role in realms traditionally reserved for the government. This is probably most readily observable in contemporary security and military affairs. Increased reliance of private contractors in the campaign in Afghanistan and Iraq is not just restricted to the support and auxiliary services, but also, as recent news reports disclose, direct combat duties as well. While this began in the Bush era as a centerpiece in former Defense Secretary Donald Rumsfeld's vision of a lean, flexible, and rapidly deployable military organization, the current Obama administration has not rolled it back (Filkins and Mazzetti 2010; Mazzetti 2010). Indeed, the same contractors continue to provide security to the State Department and

Central Intelligence Agency employees, gather intelligence, and sometimes provide direct combat assistance to the beleaguered U.S. forces.

The advent of "risk wars" since September 11 also entailed significant shift of culture, politics, and governance in the western European and North American nations. The overall import of a climate of fear and suspicion has potentially serious consequences for the governance of democratic societies. Basic civic rights of privacy and conducting one's affairs unimpeded by governmental intrusion have become some of the first collateral casualties of this new form of war.

THE CULTURE OF DISTRUST

While probably most people will agree that the threat of terror is indeed present, this should not cloud analytical judgment about the ways the threat of terror is constructed through the institutional practices of security agencies. There is little doubt that there are organizations and individuals with or without affiliation to Al-Qaeda who seek to inflict harm on the governments and citizens of many nations across the globe. However, the mere existence of these entities does not necessarily translate into a real and tangible threat. At any given moment, there are probably many people with harmful intentions to others, but that does not necessarily make them a threat, or all of them a threat of equal magnitude. In some cases, the possibility of threats has been overstated, sometimes for political purposes (Baker 2009).

During the Cold War, regardless of the enormity of the threat, the enemy was a known entity, and expected to behave within the grim yet rational paradigm of "mutually assured destruction." Unlike wars of the past, the contemporary campaigns against terrorism do not take place between uniformed military forces of contending nations. The threat of terrorism defies the separation between military and civilian personnel, and thus the traditional rules of warfare are supplanted by the logic of counterinsurgency, which seeks to identify potential threats and neutralize them with preemptive security measures. Everyone is a potential terrorist, and the burden of proof for innocence now lies with the citizenry who face threats to their lives and livelihood from both the terrorists and the security apparatuses of the state. This could well result in the death of democracy, according to Beck, since states would form alliances against their own citizens entangling everyone in a global net of suspicion. The fluidity of the category of the "enemy" creates the conditions for armed intervention without formal declaration of war against territories across the board, but also establishes a permanent warlike situation that allows states to establish a state of emergence within its own boundaries in the name of "homeland security" (2005, 13).

A "state of exception," as Agamben calls it, has defined much of the politics within and between nations since the declaration of the global war on terror (Agamben 2005). Not only does this state of semi-permanent emergency permeate the institutions and practices of contemporary governance, but it also has profound consequences for the lives of people living in ostensibly free societies. The contemporary international relations take on the form of a global civil war, which destabilizes the consensus underlined by countless international agreements since the Treaty of Westphalia. Agamben specifically cites the example of the PATRIOT Act in the United States, which gives the government the right to indefinitely incarcerate people perceived to be threat, or an "enemy combatant." These individuals represent an interstitial legal category of "detainees." They are neither subject to the rules established by the Geneva Convention nor have the due process rights of the domestic U.S. laws (Agamben 2005, 3–4).

The search for security from sometimes imaginary sources of possible harm has underlined the governance of liberal democracies in recent times. This often leads to the subversion of the very principles that these governments seek to uphold. Ericson argues that the "precautionary logic" of security against unknown and unmanageable threats could be subversive to the very foundations of democratic society, culture, and law. It results in a society based on a collective state of suspicion and unease, and a government where the security against catastrophic threats may supersede all other purposes. This logic of governance may lead to the development of "counterlaws" that often go against the very principles of constitutional legality, or new forms of surveillance that subvert all possible oversights and checks and balances that have hitherto controlled the exercise of governmental authority. Counter-laws attempt to provide a sense of security and confidence even though governmental authority may be uncertain and severely challenged by these real or perceived threats (Ericson 2007, 24).

The indefinite detention of suspects without due process this way signifies a deployment of state power that is unrestricted by the procedural safeguards put in place over many generations of democratic jurisprudence. Judith Butler claims that some of the legal and administrative maneuvers of the U.S. administration since September 11 has led to an effective suspension of the rule of law. The campaign against terrorism has established a system of government that works beyond the constitutional restrictions and established a security apparatus that have usurped the authority of incarcerating people indefinitely without probable cause or any other forms of legal justification (Butler 2004, 51). Agamben's characterization of the nature of security in the contemporary era resonates strongly with Ericson and Butler, as he argues that the contemporary regime of national security has systematically gutted the substantive and procedural laws of democratic governance without compunction—all in the name of upholding the rule of law (2005, 87).

The threat of homegrown terrorism in a multicultural society presents a whole new set of problems that have been acutely felt in recent times. The goal of preventing another attack necessarily entails enhanced vigilance by the security and law enforcement agencies. However, this also results in a state of collective surveillance and consequent suspicion of immigrant communities, which adds to the problems of integration in these societies already fraught with racial and ethnic tensions. In spite of being a settler colony, and then a nation of immigrants, migration has been the subject of considerable controversy in the United States. The perceived economic threat of migration and consequent demonization of illegal immigrants have been a mainstay of the political discourse, not only of the far right, but also increasingly more and more mainstream in the current economic climate.

In this cultural atmosphere of anxiety, distrust, and fear, the threat of terrorism adds a whole new dimension to the debates on immigration. The reorganization of immigration enforcement agencies in the Department of Homeland Security, as well as a number of other measures, has increasingly subsumed immigration into the security and counter-terror apparatuses of the state. Individuals coming from a select group of nations suspected of harboring terrorists have been required to go through a special registration process with the Department of Homeland Security. Other similar policies—such as Voluntary Interview programs for citizens of predominantly Muslim nations, Operation Liberty Shield, or the detention of asylum seekers pending adjudication, not to mention the scores of arrests and detention of immigrants immediately following the attacks—have made immigration policy an extension of national security policy (Tumlin 2004). The policies of the Department of Homeland Security and the Department of Justice of the Bush administration have added an ethos of "suspect by national origin" to immigration policy.

The contemporary campaign against terrorism has reshaped the politics and society in the nation. While surveillance, racial and ethnic profiling, and detention are hardly new in this nation's history, the U.S. government in the post–September 11 era reached a new height in the extensive and nonchalant violations of civil liberties and edicts of procedural justice which were put in place after decades of struggle. What is most striking in this period is the collusion and complicity of major political actors and institutions, as well as the unusual servility and compliance of the general population in the federal government's extensive violation of democratic conventions. As the recent political history of the United States has shown, the government has managed to mobilize popular opinion in favor of enlargement of police powers in the name of security. This mobilization of support was undoubtedly helped by the burning images of the carnage fresh in the minds of the people in the time immediately following the attacks.[5] However, public support for the overbearing authoritarianism inherent in subsequent security policies has a lot to do with the construction of a narrative that depicted the problem of terrorism as not only an existential struggle between good and evil but also an omnipresent threat to the lives of the people in the nation (Croft 2006). While the event was real in all its horror, governmental response to the attack skillfully wove together the disparate sentiments of fear, patriotism, and the desire for order. An authoritarian discourse of homeland security has emerged and thrived in a cultural climate of perennial mistrust and eternal vigilance.

NOTES

1. The Uniting and Strengthening America by Providing Appropriate Tools Required to Intercept and Obstruct Terrorism Act of 2001.
2. In its original form it also included a provision to forbid the recipients from disclosing the receipt of such letters. However, this was declared to be unconstitutional and in violation of the First and Fourth Amendments by the U.S. District Court for the Southern District of New York in *ACLU V. Ashcroft*, 2004.
3. This has been struck down by a Federal District Court in Portland, Oregon, in September 2007 for violating the Fourth Amendment in a case resulting from the arrest of a Portland area attorney.
4. The federal government to a large extent underwrites homeowner's insurance for damage due to flood and other natural disasters in the United States.
5. There has been a significant erosion of popular confidence on the government's ability to provide security against terrorism since the early days of War on Terrorism (Penn et al. 2009).

Conclusion

The Vigilant New World: Science, Law, and the Policing of Threats

There has been a renewed interest in the representation of crime and criminals among criminologists in recent times. Taking theoretical and methodological inspiration from the constructivist traditions in sociology, a large body of research in criminology has examined the institutions, actors, and processes of criminalization (Goode and Ben-Yehuda 1994a, 1994b; Jenkins 1992). By focusing on specific "moral panics" or "moral crusades," these studies analyze the epistemological and ontological dimensions of criminalization and the creation of deviant subjectivities as well as the institutional framework that creates and sustains these processes (Ackland 1995; Becker 1963; Cohen 1972; Duster 1970; Fishman 1978; Gusfield 1967; Reinarman and Levine 1997). A great percentage of these studies have focused on media representations of crime given the salience of the images of crime in popular culture in contemporary times (Anderson 1995; Bailey and Hale 1998; Barak 1994; Chermak 1997; Howit 1998; Mason 2003; Sparks 1992).

While much has been said about the cultural construction of deviance, danger, and risk, there is relatively little analysis of the scientific and legal analysis of these concepts. Crime control being one of the most important areas of the state action, the nexus between science and law in articulating the conceptions of criminal danger or risk highlights the intermingling of knowledge and power in the governance of modern societies. When it comes to construction of a distinctive subject position of the criminal, we can see how the specific legal-ethical concepts of deviance are coarticulated with the scientific concepts of normal and pathological human behavior. In other words, the deviant subjects are often hybrid concepts created simultaneously from scientific as well as legal discourses and practices.

The definition of criminal acts is shaped by legal discourses, but "crime" and "danger"/"risk" of crime are analytically distinct categories. The canons of Western law defines crime on the basis of the principle of *actus reus*, or a clear and demonstrable proof of an act of violation of law. When it comes to the conceptions of danger or risk of crime, there is no actual violation, only a possibility of one. It requires the support of a powerful and coherent system of ideas in order to convincingly render this possibility of crime into a reality and to turn humans into criminogenic dangers without any overt action on their part.

For much of history, religious discourses have governed the conceptions of morality and provided the rationale for witch hunts against heretics and misfits whose mere existence was often seen as a moral threat. In the nineteenth century, new ways of conceptualizing criminal danger came with secularization and the growing influence of sciences in understanding human behavior. The developments in behavioral sciences throughout the nineteenth century allowed early criminologists to creatively use heuristic tools from these disciplines and use them to study the problematic of crime. These constituted the major institutional discourses for the production of danger/risk that rendered these conceptual artifices into real and tangible entities, and created what Foucault has called a "regime of truth" (Foucault 1980, 131). Given the epistemological spirit of the age, scientific positivism became the preferred choice for early criminologists. New conceptions of criminal danger developed in the nineteenth century as embodied by specific types of potential offenders. The guilt of these individuals did not have to be manifested in concrete criminal acts, but rather in the possibility of such acts and the risk this posed to the society. This sought to radically revise the conception of criminal responsibility by emphasizing the existence of certain criminals whose very existence was a threat to the society regardless of whether they committed an actual act of violation or harm.

Two distinct concepts of innate criminal danger developed in the nineteenth century that influenced the dominant trends of criminological research in the early twentieth century. One of these focused on heritable intellectual deficiency as a predictor of behavioral delinquency. There were two different traditions within this school of thought. Criminal anthropologists following Cesare Lombroso utilized concepts and techniques from evolutionary biology, anthropology, and phrenology in order to posit the existence of natural criminals marked by stigmata signifying atavism. Galton and his followers in the United Kingdom and the United States developed the new science of eugenics, and sought to unravel the mysteries of the evolutionary process that would allow for the identification and control of deviant or otherwise "unfit" individuals. This tradition was very influential in the early twentieth century during the height of the eugenic movement. However, it was later debunked by scientists and fell out of favor, especially since the disclosure of eugenic experimentations of the Nazi regime (Black 2004; Lifton 2000; Weindling 2005). The second concept of criminal danger propagated by medical professionals, psychologists, and "alienists" in France identified pathological conditions of the mind leading to "moral insanity" as the principal source of innate criminality. This school has proved to be more resilient, as theories of psychopathology or sociopathy in the twentieth century are based on this idea in varying degrees.

In the United States, the invention of the category of "defective delinquents" demonstrates the creative symbiosis of scientific knowledge as well as legal discourse and practices. The concept of feeblemindedness at the core of eugenic theories of crime posited that innate heritable mental deficiency was a predictor of moral deficiency and hence criminal behavior. The category of defective delinquent came through the fusion of a legal idea—danger of criminality—and a scientific idea—heritable psychological disability. The scientific and legal agendas of the eugenicists, social reformers, and criminal justice professionals were based on the notion of *presumed guilt* for a certain category of people whose psychological and physiological defects were seen as a predictor of delinquent behavior. Contemporary scientists and criminal justice professionals contended that the peril of the feebleminded necessitated the introduction of institutional measures that would segregate and confine these pathological individuals to protect normal citizens. By postulating the innate danger to the society posed by the "feebleminded" or "defective delinquents," the eugenic advocates called for social control measures that assigned guilt on the basis of expert scientific opinion, rather than actual criminal action. The right to equality before law for these individuals was thereby suspended in favor of the duty of the government to secure safety of its normal and productive citizens. The measures adopted to achieve this goal were not necessarily seen as punitive but rather as paternalistic, which ensured not only public safety but also the security of these individuals.

The construction of defective delinquency would give way to the idea of the psychopathic individual later with the rise of dynamic psychiatry. The concept of psychopathology was rooted in the idea of moral insanity that was developed by psychiatrists in nineteenth-century France. The new currents in contemporary criminal psychiatry provided a revisionist view of the problem of crime, especially with reference of the overemphasis on feeblemindedness. Indeed, some argued that it was important to recognize the influence of a multitude of factors, including constitutional, psychological, and environmental circumstances that afflict the human condition. These psychiatrists challenged the hereditary determinism inherent in eugenic theories, and, as an alternative, posited a more fluid notion of psychological disorders. The dynamic paradigm stressed the possibility of acquisition of pathological behavioral patterns in the life of the individual patient through trauma, lack of a nurturing family environment, and unwholesome environment. Rather than inadequacy or underdevelopment of mental faculties that supposedly characterized the feebleminded individuals, the psychopathic perspective focused on the acquired mental disorders, which impaired the moral judgment of patient/criminals. As dynamic psychiatry supplanted the organicism of eugenicist psychiatry, the image of the feebleminded delinquent or "moral imbecile" was replaced by the new image of criminal as a psychopathic individual.

The sexual psychopath and involuntary commitment statutes institutionalized psychiatric expertise in the assessment of potential danger. Since the early 1960s, clinical assessment of potential for violent behavior and psychopathological tendencies became increasingly common in the criminal justice system in the United States. Many scholars voiced concerns regarding this development and argued that the concept of danger was often tainted by subjective judgments, and, in spite of due diligence to the procedures, the risk of false diagnosis always looms large with clinical predictions of behavior. Serious challenges to psychiatric authority and the nexus between psychiatry, judiciary, and penal institutions came in the late 1960s. Contemporary cultural atmosphere, radical politics, and the rise of civil rights movements contributed to the process.

In our time, purely clinical diagnosis of danger has become increasingly supplanted with actuarial methods of risk assessment that influences sentencing and parole decisions. The old ideals of rehabilitation have largely given way to a grim realism centering on incapacitation of actual and potential criminals, and managing the problem of crime through selective incarceration of "risky" sections of the population. This development redefines the fundamental precepts of justice in a democratic society. Indeed, some may claim that democratic governance in our time is based on exclusionary strategies of social control that skillfully manipulate anxieties and fear of the people in order to legitimize its authoritarian inclinations.

This trend is very clearly discernible in periodic campaigns against political threats as well. The history of surveillance and control of political threats shows that tolerance for dissent and opposition has its limits in democratic polities. In most of these cases, the processes of assigning alleged danger have operated from the confines of the cloaks of state secrecy. These have not been subject to discussion or debate in the public sphere, nor are these established by scientific research—guilt by suspicion or association has often been the key operational principle of these campaigns. While the activities of the HCUA have gained historic infamy, such campaigns did not begin or end with the McCarthy era. It is even possible to detect echoes of those events and slogans in contemporary politics. The whipping up of public fear and hysteria regarding impending doom from the insidious machinations of people or groups labeled as Communist/socialist/terrorist should not be all that unfamiliar to anyone following American politics over the last few years.

The rise of the homeland security state since the events of September 11, 2001, has significantly altered the administration of criminal justice. We are currently living through a new era of law enforcement when traditional duties of police agencies have been expanded to include a whole range of anti-terror activities. The enormity of security measures over the last nine years is indeed a new and worrisome development to many. Additionally, a public culture of suspicion attempting to drown doubt and dissent in a climate of fear and loathing of an unknown (and often unknowable) enemy has been a hallmark of contemporary politics. Historical wisdom demonstrates that there has been an authoritarian undercurrent in the democratic institutions of governance in this nation. Past campaigns against political threats have overturned procedural safeguards of individual liberties and civil rights time and again. However, it is also the lesson of history that there have been backlashes against governmental overreach, and the periodic anti-subversive crusades have been reined in—though sometimes after destroying the careers and livelihoods of many.

The threat of radical Islam has been localized into ethnic and religious communities. Indeed, there have been widespread reports of ethnic profiling against people of West or South Asian background (Tirman 2004). Immigration has now emerged as a corollary to national security, and been subsumed under the institutional rubric of homeland security. The traditional integrative ideals of the "melting pot" or the more contemporary concepts of multiculturalism are increasingly challenged by the rise of terrorism-related threats and the widespread suspicion of immigrants. The new immigration law passed by the Arizona legislature in April 2010 could be seen as a logical extension of the "suspect until proved otherwise" ethos of some contemporary law enforcement policies. History shows us that while the post–September 11 policies and practices regarding immigration is a new development, periodic public campaigns against immigrants (whether as bootleggers, sexual deviants, drug dealers, or radical socialists and anarchists) have been present in American politics for more than a century now.

In spite of the heightened alert on people of specific ethnic background, the campaign against terrorism continues to be defined by the generalized nature of the threat. The focus of surveillance and other counter-terrorism measures continues to be expansive and all embracing. The objective of surveillance is not solely to gather information from individuals suspected of being related to terrorist activities, to apprehend them, or disrupt an impending attack. Rather, proactive measures of surveillance flow through the body social in order to seek out and identify individuals who may (or may not) have done something suggestive of a possible security risk, however peripheral it may be. The scope and range of the surveillance practices undertaken by government agencies since the terrorist attacks have not yet been subject to public scrutiny, mired as it is in the institutional secrecy that defines the nature of state security apparatuses. From whatever have been disclosed, it appears very likely that these measures far transcend such previous operations and are hardly limited to specific individuals or groups with clear links to the perpetrators of the attacks. The measures against terrorism enjoyed a significant amount of support from the people traumatized by the events. The lack of transparency about these has prevented any sustained mobilization against the potentially dangerous effects these might have on the civil society. However, it is also important to remember that while these have been exacerbated since the declaration of War on Terrorism, such technologies of security far predate the events of September 11. Indeed, presidential decision directives on national security policy beyond any kind of judicial or legislation review go all the way back to the Truman administration. A recent example of this is the National Special Security Events designation established during the Clinton administration, which federalized the security measures undertaken in important social, economic, and political events. Along with political conventions and international summits, meetings of multilateral organizations are also covered by this designation. This often had a chilling effect on even peaceful protest and demonstrations (Bajc 2007; Mitchell and Staeheli 2005; Nanes 2005).

The post–September 11 developments have led to a growing realization (and, perhaps, a resigned acceptance) of the ubiquity of surveillance technologies (Haggerty and Gazso 2005). However, these have been around for a long time (Lyon 1994; Monahan 2006; Rule et al. 1983; Staples 1998). Contemporary Western nations have been called societies of surveillance, and the overall object and scope of surveillance transcend specific threat perceptions. Monitoring of security threats is certainly not new, and the history of state security agencies, especially of the FBI under Hoover, provides ample examples of the fragility of civil liberties and right of political dissent throughout the twentieth century. However, the art and science of political surveillance has transformed significantly over time. Electronic surveillance equipment facilitates the monitoring of all forms of communications, and DNA databases and biometric technology provide ever-expanding storage for information on individual citizens by fixing identity to innate biological markers.

These examples may seem to be harbingers of a dystopic future of centralization and concentration of surveillance powers in the hand of an omnipotent and omnipresent state. But the contemporary culture of vigilance far surpasses the purview and scope of a single institution, and spreads across the social space with multiple agents, targets, and sources of surveillance (Lyon 1994). This is an essential part of what Michel Foucault has identified as "governmentality," or the techniques of governance in modern societies that are targeted at the surveillance and control of national populations (Foucault 1991). This subtle form of power seeks to control the citizenry without the overt exercise of coercion, and critically hinges on the continuous monitoring of the population in order stave off potential threats to the social order. The contemporary proliferation of surveillance technology goes beyond the purview of governments, and in many cases the initiative comes from the private sector—as evidenced by the ubiquity of closed-circuit cameras in shopping malls, department stores, and even in city streets. The objective of surveillance is not always sinister or related to control of potential security risks. Voluminous databases, whether maintained by the government agencies or commercial entities, store a variety of information about citizens—be it on consumer preferences, health or educational information, creditworthiness, or communication records. It is a truism to suggest that revolutions in information technology have fundamentally transformed our world—but it has done so in curious ways. While contemporary developments in technology have had democratizing effect on access and use of information, it has paradoxically also made people more vulnerable to the prying eyes of corporations and governments.

These are especially troubling for citizens in a democratic society, as they come with very serious concerns about privacy and civil liberties. Past experience shows that institutionalized suspicion and surveillance of potential threats to the social order have proved detrimental to the principles of democracy. Some of these technologies of governance stem from the perceived institutional need of assessing future trends and controlling potential hazards. In a number of ways, this harkens to the metaphor of iron cage so evocatively used by Weber to describe the future of capitalism. The technocratic logic of rational administration is an intrinsic part of modern state institutions. However, it is often in conflict with the substantive rationality of a democratic system of governance.

Bibliography

Ackland, C. R. 1995. *Youth, Murder and Spectacle: The Cultural Politics of "Youth in Crisis."* Boulder, CO: Westview.

Adams, Graham. 1966. *The Age of Industrial Violence, 1910–1915: The Activities and Findings of the U.S. Commission on Industrial Relations*. New York: Columbia University Press.

Adler, Herman. 1917. "A Psychiatric Contribution to the Study of Delinquency." *Journal of the American Institute of Criminal Law and Criminology* 8(1): 45–68.

Agamben, Giorgio. 2005. *State of Exception*. Chicago: University of Chicago Press.

American Psychiatric Association (APA). 1974. Clinical Aspects of the Violent Individual: A Report of the American Psychiatric Association Task Force. Washington, DC: American Psychiatric Association.

Anderson, David C. 1995. *Crime and the Politics of Hysteria: How the Willie Horton Story Changed American Justice*. New York: Times Books.

Andrew, Christopher. 1995. *For the President's Eyes Only: Secret Intelligence and American Presidency from Washington to Bush*. New York: Harper Collins.

Appignanesi, Lisa. 2008. *Mad, Bad and Sad: Women and the Mind Doctors*. New York: W. W. Norton and Co.

Aradau, Claudia, and Rens Van Munster. 2007. "Governing Terrorism Through Risk: Taking Precautions, (Un)Knowing the Future." *European Journal of International Relations* 13(1): 89–115.

Augstein, Hannah Franziska. 1996. "J. C. Prichard's Concept of Moral Insanity—A Medical Theory of the Corruption of Human Nature." *Medical History* 40: 311–443.

Bailey, F. Y., and D. C Hale (eds.). 1998. *Popular Culture, Crime and Justice*. Belmont, CA: Wadsworth Press.

Bajc, Vida. 2007. "Surveillance in Public Rituals: Security Meta-ritual and the 2005 U.S. Presidential Inauguration." *American Behavioral Scientist* 50(12): 1648–73.

Baker, Peter. 2009. "Bush Official, in Book, Tells of Pressure on '04 Vote."*New York Times*, August 20, 2009. Accessed from www.nytimes.com/2009/08/21/us/21ridge.html?_r=1&ref=tom_ridge, June 30, 2010.

Ballantine, Henry W. 1919. "Criminal Responssibility of the Insane and the Feeble-minded." *Journal of American Institute of Criminal Law and Criminology* 9(4): 485–99.

Barak, Gregg. 1994. *Media, Process, and the Social Construction of Crime: Studies in Newsmaking Criminology*. New York: Garland Publishers.

———. 2004. "A Reciprocal Approach to Terrorism and Terrorist-like Behavior." Pp. 33–49 in Matthew Deflem (ed.), *Terrorism and Counter-Terrorism: Criminological Perspectives*. Amsterdam: Elsevier.

Beck, Ulrich. 1992. *Risk Society: Towards a New Modernity*. London: Sage.

———. 1999. *World Risk Society Revisited*. Cambridge: Blackwell.

———. 2002. "The Terrorist Threat: The World Risk Society Revisited." *Theory, Culture and Society* 19(4): 389–55.

———. 2005. *Power in the Global Age*. Cambridge: Polity Press.

———. 2009. *The World at Risk*. Cambridge: Polity Press.

Becker, Herbert. 1963. *Outsiders: Studies in the Sociology of Deviance*. New York: Free Press.

Beirne, Piers. 1993. *Inventing Criminology: Essays on the Rise of Homo Criminalis*. Albany: State University of New York Press.

Berrios, G. E. 1996. *The History of Mental symptoms: Descriptive Psychopathology since the Nineteenth Century*. Cambridge: Cambridge University Press.

Bicchi, Federica, and Mary Martin. 2006. "Talking Tough or Talking Together? European Security Discourses towards the Mediterranean." *Mediterranean Politics* 11(2): 189–207.

Bigo, Didier. 2002. "Security and Immigration: Toward a Critique of the Governmentality of Unease." *Alternatives* 27: 63–92.

Binet, Alfred. 1911a. "La mesure developpement de l'intelligence chez les jeunes enfants." *Bulletin de la Societe libre pour l'Etude psychologique de l'Enfant* 10 and 11: 187–248.

———. 1911b. "Nouvelles recherches sur la mesure d'un niveau intellectuel chez les enfants d'école." *L'Année psychologique* 17: 145–201.

Binet, Alfred, and Theodore Simon. 1905. "Méthodes nouvelles pour diagnostic du niveau intellectual des anormaux." *L'Anee psychologique* 11: 191–244.

———. 1908. "Le development de l'intelligence chez enfants." *L'Anee psychologique* 14: 1–94.

———. 1909. "L'intelligence des imbeciles." *L'Anee psychologique* 15: 1–147.

Black, Edwin. 2004. *War Against the Weak: Eugenics and America's Campaign to Create a Master Race*. New York: Thunder's Mouth.

Blackstock, Nelson. 1988. *COINTELPRO: The FBI's Secret War on Political Freedom*. New York: Pathfinder.

Bladin, Peter. 2001. *A Disease Once Sacred: A History of the Medical Understanding of Epilepsy*. Montrouge, France: John Libbey Eurotext.

Blasi, Vincent. 1988. "First Amendment and the Ideal of Civic Courage: The Brandeis Opinion in *Whitney v. California*." *William and Mary Law Review* 29: 653.

Bleuler, Eugen. 1951 (1911). *Dementia Praecox; or The Group of Schizophrenias* (trans. Joseph Zinkin). London: Allen and Unwin.

Borden, Howard G. 1924. "Factors for Predicting Parole Success." *Journal of the American Institute of Criminal Law and Criminology* 19(3): 328–36.

Boston, Charles A. 1913. "A Protest against Laws Authorizing Sterilization of Criminals and Imbeciles." *Journal of the American Institute of Criminal Law and Criminology* 4(3): 326–58.

Boyne, Shane. 2004. "Law, Terrorism, and Social Movements: The Tension Between Politics and Security in Germany's Anti-Terrorism Legislation." *Cardozo Journal of International and Comparative Law* 41(12): 41–59.

Brace, Charles Loring. 1872. *The Dangerous Classes of New York and Twenty Years' Work Among Them*. New York: Wynkoop & Hallenbeck.

Braithwaite, John. 2000. "The New Regulatory State and the Transformation of Criminology." *British Journal of Criminology* 40(2): 228–38.

Brandeis, Louis D. 1927. "Concurrence: *Whitney v. California*." U.S. Supreme Court, 274 U.S. 357.

British Parliament. 2006. *The Terrorism Act of 2006*. London: The Stationary Office.

Broehl, Wayne G. 1964. *The Molly Maguires*. Cambridge, MA: Harvard University Press.

Burgess, Ernest W. 1928. "Factors Determining Success or Failure on Parole." In A. A. Bruce (ed.), *The Workings of the Indeterminate Sentence Law and the Parole System in Illinois*. Montclair, NJ: Patterson Smith, 1968.

Butler, Judith. 2004. *Precarious Life: The Powers of Mourning and Violence*. London: Verso.

Carey, Allison. 2003. "Beyond the Medical Model: A Reconsideration of 'Feeblemindedness,' Citizenship, and Eugenic Restrictions." *Disability and Society* 18(4): 411–30.

Carlson, Elof Axel. 2001. *The Unfit: A History of a Bad Idea*. Cold Spring Harbor, NY: Cold Spring Harbor Laboratory Press.

Carpentar, William B. 1883. *Principles of Mental Physiology with Their Applications to the Training and Discipline of the Mind and the Study of Its Morbid Conditions*. New York: D. Appleton and Company.

Carroll, Thomas F. 1920. "Freedom of Speech and of the Press in the Federalist Period: The Sedition Act." *Michigan Law Review* 18(7): 615–51.
Carruthers, Bruce G., and Wendy Nelson Espeland. 1991. "Accounting for Rationality: Doubleentry Bookkeeping and the Rhetoric of Economic Rationality." *American Journal of Sociology* 97(1): 31–69.
Castel, Robert. 1991. "From Dangerousness to Risk." Pp. 281–98 in Graham Burchell, Colin Gordon, and Peter Miller (eds.), *The Foucault Effect*. Chicago: University of Chicago Press.
Cattell, James McKeen. 1890. "Mental Tests and Measurements." *Mind* 15: 373–88.
Chafee, Zechariah. 1919. "Freedom of Speech in Wartime." *Harvard Law Review* 32(8): 932–73.
———. 1950. "The Registration of 'Communist-Front' Organizations in the Mundt-Nixon Bill." *Harvard Law Review* 63(8): 1382–90.
———. 1964. *Free Speech in the United States*. Cambridge, MA: Harvard University Press.
Chermak, Steven. 1997. *Victims in the News: Crime and American News Media*. Boulder, CO: Westview Press.
Churchill, Ward, and Jim Vander Wall. 2002. *The COINTELPRO Papers: Documents from FBI's Secret War against Dissent in the United States*, second edition. Cambridge, MA: South End Press.
Cleckley, Hervey. 1941. *The Mask of Sanity: An Attempt to Reinterpret the So-called Psychopathic Personality*. St. Louis: C. V. Mosby Company.
Coben, Stanley. 1963. *A. Mitchell Palmer: Politician*. New York: Columbia University Press.
Cohen, Stanley. 1972. *Folk Devils and Moral Crusades*. London: MacGibbon and Kee.
Commonwealth of Massachusetts. 1922. *The Massachusetts Laws Relating to Insane Persons and Other Classes under the Supervision of Department of Mental Diseases*. Boston: Wright, Potter Printing Company.
Conrad, John P., and Simon Dinitz. 1978. *In Fear of Each Other*. Lexington, MA: Lexington Books.
Cotter, Cornelius P., and J. Malcolm Smith. 1957. "An American Paradox: The Emergency Detention Act of 1950." *Journal of Politics* 19(1): 20–33.
Cowan, Ruth Schwartz. 1974. "Francis Galton's Statistical Ideas: The Influence of Eugenics." *Isis* 63(4): 509–28.
Coxe, Warren W. 1916. "Grading Intelligence by Years and Points." *Journal of the American Institute of Criminal Law and Criminology* 7(3): 341–65.
Crabtree, Adam. 2003. "Automatism and the Emergence of Dynamic Psychiatry." *Journal of the History of the Behavioral Sciences* 39(1): 51–70.
Cram, Ian. 2009. *Terror and the War on Dissent: Freedom of Expression in the Age of Al Qaeda*. New York: Springer.
Croft, Stuart. 2006. *Culture, Crisis and America's War on Terror*. Cambridge: Cambridge University Press.
Cunningham, David. 2004. *There's Something Happening Here: The New Left, The Klan, and FBI Counterintelligence*. Berkeley: University of California Press.
Cuthbert, Norma Barrett. 1949. *Lincoln and the Baltimore Plot: From Pinkerton Records and Related Papers*. San Marino, CA: Huntington Library.
Daily, Elizabeth G. 2006. "Beyond Persons, Houses, Papers, and Effects: Rewriting the Fourth Amendment for National Security Surveillance." *Lewis and Clark Law Review* 10(3): 641–71.
Darwin, Charles. 1905 (1871). *The Descent of Man*. New York: P. F. Collier and Sons.
Davenport, Charles B. 1909. "The Influence of Heredity in Human Society." *Annals of the American Academy of Political and Social Science* 34(1): 16–21.
———. 1921. "Research in Eugenics." *Science: New Series* 54(400): 391–97.
Davis, James Kirkpatrick. 1992. *Spying on America: The FBI's Domestic Counterintelligence Program*. Westport, CT: Praeger.

———. 1997. *Assault on the Left: The FBI and the Sixties Antiwar Movement.* Westport, CT: Praeger.
De Boismont, A. Brierre. 1871. "The Criminal Insane of England: A Medico-psychological and Legal Study." *American Journal of Insanity* 27: 278–308.
De Quirós, C. Bernaldo. 1912. *Modern Theories of Criminality* (trans. Alfonso De Salvio). Boston: Little, Brown and Co.
Dershowiz, Alan. 1969. "The Psychiatrist's Power in Civil Commitment." *Psychology Today* 2: 43–47.
———. 1974. "Dangerousness as a Criterion for Confinement." *Bulletin of the American Academy of Psychiatry and Law* 11: 172–79.
———. 1978. "The Role of Psychiatry in the Sentencing Process." *International Journal of Law and Psychiatry* 1: 63–78.
Despine, Prosper. 1868. *Psychologie naturelle: Étude sur les facultés intellectuelles et morales.* Paris: F. Savy.
———. 1875. *De la folie au point de vue philosophique, ou plus spécialement psychologique.* Paris: F. Savy.
Dewees, F. P. 1877. *Molly Maguires: Origin, Growth and the Character of the Organization.* Philadelphia: J. P. Lippincott and Company.
Dewey, John. 1900. "Psychology and Social Practice." *Psychological Review* 7: 105–24.
Diamond, Bernard L. 1956. "Issac Ray and the Trial of Daniel M'Naghten." *American Journal of Psychiatry* 112: 651–56.
———. 1974. "The Psychiatric Prediction of Dangerousness." *University of Pennsylvania Law Review* 123(2): 439–52.
Dix, George. 1980. "Clinical Evaluation of the 'Dangerousness' of 'Normal' Criminal Defendants." *Virginia Law Review* 66(3): 523–81.
Donner, Frank J. 1980. *The Age of Surveillance: The Aims and Methods of America's Political Intelligence System.* New York: Alfred A. Knopf.
Donovan, Brian. 2003. "The Sexual Basis of Racial Formation: Anti-Vice Activism and the Creation of the Twentieth-Century Color Line." *Ethnic and Racial Studies* 26(4): 708–28.
Dorn, Nicholas, and Michael Levi. 2006. "Regulation of Insurance and Corporate Security: Integrating Crime and Terrorism Seriousness into the Analysis." *European Journal of Criminal Policy Research* 12(3–4): 527–77.
Douglas, Mary. 1966. *Purity and Danger: An Analysis of Concepts of Pollution and Taboo.* New York: Routledge.
———. 1992. *Risk and Blame: Essays in Cultural Theory.* New York: Routledge.
———. 1997. "The Depoliticization of Risk." Pp. 121–32 in Richard J. Ellis and Michael Thompson (eds.), *Culture Matters: Essays in Honor of Aaron Wildavsky.* Boulder, CO: Westview.
Douglas, Mary, and Aaron B. Wildavsky. 1982. *Risk and Culture: An Essay on the Selection of Technical and Environmental Dangers.* Berkeley: University of California Press.
Dowbiggin, Ian R. 1991. *Inheriting Madness: Professionalization and Psychiatric Knowledge in Nineteenth Century France.* Berkeley: University of California Press.
Dugdale, Robert L. 1910 (1876). *The Jukes: A Study in Crime, Pauperism, Diseases and Heredity.* New York: G. P. Putnam's Sons.
Dunbar, Leslie W. 1951. "Beyond Korematsu: The Emergency Detention Act of 1950." *University of Pittsburgh Law Review* 13: 221.
Duster, Troy. 1970. *Legislation of Morality: Law, Drugs and Moral Judgment.* New York: Free Press.
Emery, James A. 1912. "Labor Organizations and the Sherman Law." *The Journal of Political Economy* 20(6): 599–612.
Ennis, Bruce J., and Thomas R. Litwack. 1974. "Psychiatry and the Presumption of Expertise: Flipping Coin in the Courtroom." *California Law Review* 62(3): 693–752.
Ericson, Richard V. 2007. *Crime in an Insecure World.* Cambridge: Polity Press.
Ericson, Richard, and Aaron Doyle. 2004. "Catastrophe Risk, Insurance and Terrorism." *Economy and Society* 33(2): 135–73.

Ericson, Richard V., and Kevin D. Haggerty. 1997. *Policing the Risk Society*. Toronto: University of Toronto Press.

Esquirol, Jean-Étienne Dominique. 1845. *Mental Maladies: Treatise on Insanity* (trans. E. K. Hunt). Philadelphia: Lea and Blanchard.

Eugenic News. 1919 (1918). "Eugenic Laws." *Journal of American Institute of Criminal Law and Criminology* 9(4): 596–97.

European Council. 2001. "Council Common Position of 27 December 2001 on Combating Terrorism." 2001/930/CFSP, Article 16.

Feeley, Malcolm, and Jonathan Simon. 1992. "The New Penology: Notes on the Emerging Strategy of Corrections and its Implications." *Criminology* 30(4): 449–74.

———. 1994. "Actuarial Justice: The Emerging New Criminal Law." Pp. 173–201 in David Nelken (ed.), *The Futures of Criminology*. London/Beverly Hills, CA: Sage Publishers.

Ferri, Enrico. 1901. *The Positive School of Criminology* (trans. Ernest Untermann). Chicago: Charles H. Kerr and Company.

———. 1917 (1883). *Criminal Sociology* (trans. Joseph I. Kelly and John Lisle). Boston: Little, Brown and Company.

Feurlicht, Roberta Strauss. 1971. *America's Reign of Terror: World War I, The Red Scare, and the Palmer Raids*. New York: Random House.

Filkins, Dexter, and Mark Mazzetti. 2010. "Contractors Tied to Efforts to Track and Kill Militants." *New York Times*, March 14, 2010. Accessed from www.nytimes.com/2010/03/15/world/asia/15contractors.html, June 30, 2010.

Finan, Christopher. 2007. *From the Palmer Raids to the Patriot Act: The History of the Fight for Free Speech in America*. Boston: Beacon Press.

Fine, Sidney. 1955. "Anarchism and the Assassination of McKinley." *American Historical Review* 60(4): 777–99.

Fishman, M. 1978. "Crime Waves as Ideology." *Social Problems* 25: 531–43.

Fleming, John G., and Bruce Maximov. 1974. "The Patient or His Victim: The Therapist's Dilemma." *California Law Review* 62: 1025–68.

Foner, Phillip S. 1975. *History of the Labor Movement in the United States, Vol. 2: From the Founding of the American Federation of Labor to the Emergence of American Imperialism*. New York: International Publishers.

———. 1980. *History of the Labor Movement in the United States, Volume V: The AFL in the Progressive Era, 1910–1915*. New York: International Publishers.

Forster, Susanne. 2009. "Control Orders: Borders to the Freedom of Movement or Moving the Borders of Freedom." Pp. 349–72 in Marianne Wade and Almir Maljevic (eds.), *A War of Terror? The European Stance on a New Threat, Changing Laws and Human Rights Implications*. New York: Springer.

Foucault, Michel. 1979. *Discipline and Punish: The Birth of the Prison*. New York: Vintage.

———. 1980. *Power/Knowledge: Selected Interviews and Other Writings 1972–77* (ed. Colin Gordon). New York: Pantheon.

———. 1982. *I, Pierre Rivière, Having Slaughtered My Mother, My Sister, and My Brother. . . : A Case of Parricide in the 19th Century*. Lincoln: University of Nebraska Press.

———. 1990. "On the Concept of the Dangerous Individual in Nineteenth-Century Psychiatric Discourse." Pp. 125–51 in Lawrence D. Kritzman (ed.), *Michel Foucault: Politics, Philosophy, Culture: Interviews and Other Writings 1977–1984*. New York: Routledge.

———. 1991. "Governmentality." Pp. 87–104 in Graham Burchell, Colin Gordon, and Peter Miller (eds.), *The Foucault Effect: Studies in Governmentality*. Chicago: University of Chicago Press.

———. 2004. *Abnormal: Lectures at the College de France, 1974–1975*. London: Macmillan.

Fox, John F. 2004. "Unique Unto Itself: The Records of the Federal Bureau of Investigation 1908 to 1945." *Journal of Government Information* 30(4): 470–81.

FPF. 1948. "The Legal Disposition of the Sexual Psychopath." *University of Pennsylvania Law Review* 9(6): 872–87.

Friedman, Morris. 1907. *Pinkerton Labor Spy*. New York: Wilshire Book Co.
Galton, Francis. 1869. *Hereditary Genius: Its Laws and Its Consequence*. New York: D. Appleton and Co.
———. 1883. *Inquiries into Human Faculty and Its Development*. London: Macmillan.
———. 1889. *Natural Inheritance*. London: Macmillan.
———. 1904. "Eugenics: Its Definition, Scope and Aims." *American Journal of Sociology* 10(1): 1–25.
———. 1905. "Studies in Eugenics." *American Journal of Sociology* 11(1): 11–25.
Garland, David. 1985. "The Criminal and His Science." *British Journal of Criminology* 25(2): 109–37.
———. 1996. "Limits of the Sovereign State: Strategies of Crime Control in Contemporary Society." *British Journal of Criminology* 36(4): 445–71.
———. 2001. *The Culture of Control: Crime and Social Order in Contemporary Society*. Chicago: University of Chicago Press.
Garofalo, Raffaele. 1914 (1885). *Criminology* (trans. Robert W. Miller). Boston: Little, Brown and Company.
Geddes, Andrew. 2003. *The Politics of Migration and Immigration in Europe*. London: Sage.
Giddens, Anthony. 1991. *Modernity and Self-Identity: Self and Society in the Late Modern Age*. Cambridge: Polity.
Gitelman, Howard M. 1988. *Legacy of the Ludlow Massacre: A Chapter in American Industrial Relations*. Philadelphia: University of Pennsylvania Press.
Glueck, Bernard. 1954. "Changing Concepts in Forensic Psychiatry." *The Journal of Criminal Law, Criminology and Police Science* 45(2): 123–32.
Glueck, Sheldon. 1927. "Psychiatric Examination of Persons Accused of Crime." *The Yale Law Journal* 36(5): 632–48.
———. 1928. "Psychiatry and Criminal Law." *Virginia Law Review* 14(3): 155–81.
Glueck, Sheldon, and Eleanor T. Glueck. 1930. *Five Hundred Criminal Careers*. New York: Knopf.
Goddard, Henry H. 1911. "Two Thousand Children Measured by the Binet-Simon Measuring Scale of Intelligence." *Pedagogical Seminary* 18: 232–59.
———. 1912. *The Kallikak Family*. New York: Macmillan.
———. 1915. *The Criminal Imbecile: An Analysis of Three Remarkable Murder Cases*. New York: Macmillan.
———. 1917. "Mental Tests and the Immigrants." *Journal of Delinquency* 2: 243–77.
Goldstein, Jan. 1991. "The Uses of Male Hysteria: Medical and Literary Discourse in Nineteenth Century France." *Representations* 34: 134–65.
———. 2002. *Console and Classify: The French Psychiatric Profession in the Nineteenth Century*. Cambridge: Cambridge University Press.
Goldstein, Joseph, and Jay Katz. 1960. "Dangerousness and Mental Illness: Some Observations on the Decision to Release Persons Acquitted by Reasons of Insanity." *Yale Law Journal* 70(2): 225–39.
Goldstein, Robert Justin. 1978. *Political Repression in Modern America: 1870 to Present*. Cambridge, MA/New York: Schenkman Publishing Co./Two Continents Publishing Group.
Gonzales, Alberto. 2005. Press Briefing by Attorney General Alberto Gonzales and General Michael Hayden, Principal Deputy Director for National Intelligence. White House, December 19, 2005. Accessed from georgewbush-whitehouse.archives.gov/news/releases/2005/12/print/20051219-1.html.
Goode, E., and Norman Ben-Yehuda. 1994a. *Moral Panics*. Cambridge, MA: Blackwill.
———. 1994b. "Moral Panics: Culture, Politics and Social Construction." *Annual Review of Sociology* 20: 149–71.
Goodman, Walter. 1968. *The Committee: The Extraordinary Career of the House Committee on Un-American Activities*. New York: Farrar Straus & Giroux.
Goring, Charles Buckman. 1913. *The English Convict: A Statistical Study*. London: HM Stationery Office/Darling and Son.

Gough, Harrison G. 1948. "A Sociological Theory of Psychopathy." *American Journal of Sociology* 53(5): 359–66.
Gould, Stephen Jay. 1981. *The Mismeasurement of Man*. New York: W. W. Norton.
Greenwood, Peter W., and Alan Abrahamse. 1982. *Selective Incapacitation*. Santa Monica, CA: Rand.
Greenwood, Peter W., and Susan Turner. 1987. *Selective Incapacitation Revisited: Why the High-rate Offenders Are Hard to Predict*. Santa Monica, CA: Rand.
Gregory, Charles. 1943. "Union Peacetime Restraints in Collective Bargaining." *The University of Chicago Law Review* 10(2): 177–92.
Griffith, Robert. 1971. "The Political Context of McCarthyism." *The Journal of Politics* 33(1): 24–35.
Grob, Gerald N. 1983. *Mental Illness and American Society, 1875–1940*. Princeton, NJ: Princeton University Press.
———. 1985. *The Inner World of American Psychiatry, 1890–1940*. New Brunswick, NJ: Rutgers University Press.
Grove, William M. 2005. "Clinical versus Statistical Predictions: The Contribution of Paul E. Meehl." *Journal of Clinical Psychiatry* 61(10): 1233–1243
Grove, William M., and Paul E. Meehl. 1996. "Comparative Efficiency of Informal (Subjective, Impressionistic) and Formal (Mechanical, Algorithmic) Prediction Procedures: The Clinical-Statistical Controversy." *Psychology, Public Policy, and Law* 2: 293–323.
Gusfield, David. 1967. "Moral Passage: The Symbolic Process in Public Designations of Deviance." *Social Problems* 15(2): 175–88.
Hacker, Frederick J., and Marcel Frym. 1955. "The Sexual Psychopath Act in Practice: A Critical Discussion." *California Law Review* 43(5): 766–80.
Hacking, Ian. 1990. *Taming of Chance*. Cambridge: Cambridge University Press.
Hagedorn, Ann. 2007. *Savage Peace: Hope and Fear in America, 1919*. New York: Simon & Schuster.
Haggerty, Kevin D., and Amber Gazso. 2005. "Seeing Beyond the Ruins: Surveillance as a Response to Terrorist Threats." *Canadian Journal of Sociology/Cahiers canadiens de sociologie* 30(2): 169–87.
Hallsworth, Simon. 2006. "Racial Targeting and Social Control: Looking Behind the Police." *Critical Criminology* 14: 293–311.
Hannah-Moffat, Kelly. 2005. "Criminogenic Needs and the Transformative Risk Subject: Hybridizations of Risk/Need in Penalty." *Punishment and Society* 7(1): 29–51.
Hare, Robert D. 1991. *The Hare Psychopathy Checklist—Revised*. Toronto: Multi Health System.
———. 1996. "Psychopathy: A Clinical Construct Whose Time Has Come." *Criminal Justice and Behavior* 23: 25–54.
Hare, Robert D., Stephen Hart, and Timothy Harpur. 1991. "Psychopathy and the DSM—IV Criteria for Antisocial Personality Disorder." *Journal of Abnormal Psychology* 100(3): 391–98.
Harris, Grant T., Marnie E. Rice, and Vernon L. Quinsey. 1993. "Violent Recidivism of Mentally Disordered Offenders: The Development of a Statistical Prediction Instrument." *Criminal Justice and Behavior* 20(4): 315–35.
Hart, Hornell. 1923. "Predicting Parole Success." *Journal of Criminal Law, Criminology and Police Science* 14(3): 405–13.
Healy, William. 1915. *The Individual Delinquent: A Text Book of Diagnosis and Prognosis for all Concerned in Understanding Offenders*. Boston: Little, Brown, and Company.
Healy, William, and Mary Tenney Healy. 1915. *Pathological Lying, Accusation, and Swindling—A Study in Forensic Psychology*. Boston: Little, Brown and Company.
Hellman, Daniel S., and Nathan Blackman. 1966. "Enuresis, Firesetting and Cruelty to Animals: A Triad Predictive of Adult Crime." *American Journal of Psychiatry* 122(12): 1431–35.
Hofstader, Richard, and Michael Wallace (eds.). 1971. *American Violence: A Documentary History*. New York: Vintage.

Hollway, Wendy, and Tony Jefferson. 1997. "The Risk Society in an Age of Anxiety: Situating Fear of Crime." *The British Journal of Sociology* 48(2): 255–66.

Hooton, Ernest A. 1939a. *The American Criminal: An Anthropological Study*. Cambridge, MA: Harvard University Press.

———. 1939b. *Crime and the Man*. Cambridge, MA: Harvard University Press.

Horan, James D. 1967. *The Pinkertons: The Detective Dynasty that Made History*. New York: Crown Publishers.

Howit, D. 1998. *Crime, the Media and the Law*. Chichester, UK: Wiley Press.

Hoyt, Edwin P. 1969. *The Palmer Raids, 1919–1920: An Attempt to Suppress Dissent*. New York: Seabury Press.

Hudson, Barbara. 2003. *Justice in the Risk Society: Challenging and Reaffirming Justice in Late Modernity*. London: Sage.

Huey, E. B. 1908. *The Psychology and Pedagogy of Reading: With a Review of the History of Reading and Writing and of Methods, Texts and Hygiene in Reading*. New York: Macmillan.

Hunt, Alan R. 1955. "Federal Supremacy and State Anti-Subversive Legislation." *Michigan Law Review* 53(3): 407–38.

Hunter, Joel D. 1914. "Sterilization of Criminals (Report of Committee H of the Institute." *Journal of American Institute of Criminal Law and Criminology* 5(4): 514–39.

Ibrahim, Maggie. 2005. "Securitization of Immigration: A Racial Discourse." *International Migration* 43(5): 163–87.

Ireland, William Witherspoon. 1877. *On Idiocy and Imbecility*. London: J. A. Churchill.

Jackson, Pamela Irving, and Roderick Parks. 2007. "Parallel Societies, Cultural Tolerance and Securitization: Muslims and Anti-Immigrant Sentiment in Western Democracies." *Journal of Social and Ecological Boundaries* 3(1): 7–42.

Jackson, William K. 1939. "Constitutional Law: Validity of Sex Offender Acts." *Michigan Law Review* 37(4): 613–25.

Jenkins, Paul. 1992. *Intimate Enemies: Moral Panics in Contemporary Britain*. Hawthorne, NY: Aldine de Gruyter.

Jensen, Joan M. 1991. *Army Surveillance in America, 1775–1980*. New Haven, CT: Yale University Press.

Jones, Kathleen W. 1999. *Taming the Troublesome Child: American Families, Child Guidance and the Limits of Psychiatric Authority*. Cambridge, MA: Harvard University Press.

Kane, Paul. 2008. "House Passes Spy Bill; Senate Expected to Follow." *Washington Post*, June 21, 2008.

Kaross, Sonia. 1989. "Palmer Raids: The Deportation Mania Begins." Pp. 159–64 in Bud Schultz and Ruth Schultz (eds.), *It Did Happen Here: Recollections of Political Repression in America*. Berkeley: University of California Press.

Karpman, Benjamin. 1941. "Perversions as Neuroses (The Paraphiliac Neuroses): Their Relation to Psychopathy and Criminality." *Journal of Criminal Psychopathology* 3: 180–199.

———. 1951. "The Sexual Psychopath." *Journal of Criminal Law, Criminology and Police Science* 42(2): 184–98.

———. 1954. *The Sexual Offender and His Offenses*. New York: Julian Press.

Karyotis, Georgios. 2007. "Europan Migration Policy in the Aftermath of September 11: The Security-Migration Nexus." *Innovation* 20(1): 1–17.

Kemper, Donald. 1965. *Decade of Fear: Senator Jennings and Civil Liberties*. Columbia: University of Missouri Press.

Kempf-Leonard, Kimberly, and Elicka Peterson. 2000. "Expanding Realms of the New Penology: The Advent of Actuarial Justice for Juveniles." *Punishment & Society* 2(1): 66–97.

Kenny, Kevin. 1998. *Making Sense of the Molly Maguires*. New York: Oxford Univerity Press.

Kessler, Mark. 1993. "Legal Discourse and Political Intolerance: The Ideology of Clear and Present Danger." *Law & Society Review* 27(3): 559–98.

Kevles, Daniel. 1985. *In the Name of Eugenics: Genetics and the Uses of Human Heredity*. New York: Alfred A. Knopf.

Kirshen, H. B. 1951. "The Internal Security Act of 1950." *Bulletin of the American Association of University Professors* 37(2): 260–75.

Kovner, Joseph. 1947. "The Legislative History of Section 6 of the Clayton Act." *Columbia Law Review* 47(5): 749–65.

Kozol, Harry L., Richard J. Boucher, and Ralph F. Garofalo. 1972. "The Diagnosis and Treatment of Dangerousness." *Crime & Delinquency* 18(4): 371–92.

Kraepelin, Emil. 1981 (1907). *Lectures in Clinical Psychiatry*. Delmar, NY: Scholars Facsimile and Reproductions.

Krafft-Ebing, Richard Von. 1928 (1898). *Psychopathia Sexualis with Especial Reference to the Antipathic Sexual Instinct: A Medico-Forensic Study, Revised Edition*. Philadelphia: Physicians and Surgeons.

Kuhlman, F. 1918. "A Further Extension and Revision of the Binet-Simon Scale." *Journal of the American Institute of Criminal Law and Criminology* 8(6): 891–901.

LaFree, Gary, and Laura Dugan. 2004. "How Does Studying Terrorism Compare to Studying Crime?" Pp. 53–74 in Matthew Deflem (ed.), *Terrorism and Counter-Terrorism: Criminological Perspectives*. Amsterdam: Elsevier.

Laughlin, Harry. 1922. *Eugenic Sterilization in the United States*. Chicago: Psychopathic Laboratory of the Municipal Court of Chicago.

Laughlin, Harry H. 1923. "Analysis of America's Modern Melting Pot." *Hearings before the Committee on Immigration and Naturalization, House of Representatives, Sixty-seventh Congress, Third Session*. November 21, 1922. Serial 7-C. Statement of Harry H. Laughlin. Washington, DC: Government Printing Office.

Lens, Sidney. 2009. *The Labor Wars: From the Molly Maguires to the Sit Downs*. Chicago: Haymarket Books.

Levinson, Richard M., and Georgeann Ramsey. 1979. "Dangerousness, Stress, and Mental Health Evaluations." *Journal of Health and Social Behavior* 20(2): 178–87.

Levy, Leonard. 1960. *Legacy of Suppression: Freedom of Speech and Press in Early American History*. Cambridge, MA: The Belknap Press of the Harvard University Press.

Lewis, Charles, and Adam Mayle. 2003. "Justice Dept. Drafts Sweeping Expansion of Anti-Terrorism Act: Center Publishes Secret Draft of 'Patriot II' Legislation." Center for Public Integrity. Accessed from www.publicintegrity.org/articles/entry/377/, April 23, 2010.

Lianos, Michaelis, and Mary Douglas. 2000. "Dangerization and the End of Deviance: The Institutional Environment." *The British Journal of Criminology* 40(2): 261–78.

Lifton, Robert J. 2000. *The Nazi Doctors: Medical Killing and the Psychology of Genocide*. New York: Basic Books.

Lilly, J. Robert. 1992. "Selling Justice: Electronic Monitoring and the Security Industry." *Justice Quarterly* 9: 493–503.

Linde, Hans A. 1970. "'Clear and Present Danger' Reexamined: Dissonance in the *Brandenburg* Concerto." *Stanford Law Review* 22(6): 1163–86.

Lindsay, Matthew. 1998. "Reproducing a Fit Citizenry: Dependency, Eugenics, and the Law of Marriage in the United States, 1860 1920." *Law and Social Inquiry* 23(3): 541–85.

Litwak, Thomas R. 2001. "Actuarial versus Clinical Assessments of Dangerousness." *Psychology, Public Policy, and Law* 7(2): 409–43.

Lodge, Juliet. 2004. "EU Homeland Security: Citizens or Suspects." *European Integration* 26(3): 253–79.

Lombroso, Cesare. 1911 (1876). *Crime: Its Causes and Remedy* (trans. Henry P. Horton). Boston: Little, Brown and Company.

Lombroso-Ferrero, Gina. 1972 (1921). *Criminal Man According to the Classification of Cesare Lombroso*. Montclair, NJ: Patterson Smith.

Longaker, Richard. 1974. "Emergency Detention: The Generation Gap, 1950–1971." *Political Research Quarterly* 27(3): 395–408.

Lunbeck, Elizabeth. 1994. *The Psychiatric Persuasion: Knowledge, Gender and Power in Modern America*. Princeton, NJ: Princeton University Press.

Lundberg, George A. 1926. "Case Work and the Statistical Method." *Social Forces* 5(1): 61–65.

———. 1941. "Case Studies versus Statistical Methods: An Issue based on Misunderstanding." *Sociometry* 4: 379–83.

Lynd, Staughton. 1975. "*Brandenburg v. Ohio*: A Speech Test for All Seasons?" *University of Chicago Law Review* 43(1): 151–91.

Lyon, David. 1994. *The Electronic Eye: The Rise of Surveillance Society*. Minneapolis: University of Minnesota Press.

MacCurdy, John T. 1916. "Review of the Individual Delinquent." *The Journal of Abnormal Psychology* 10: 374–79.

MacDonald, John M. 1967. "Homicidal Threats." *American Journal of Psychiatry* 124(4): 475–82.

Malmquist, Carl P. 1971. "Premonitory Signs of Homicidal Aggression in Juveniles." *American Journal of Psychiatry* 128(4): 461–65.

Mansfield, Harvey C. 1941. "The Legislative Veto and the Deportation of Aliens." *Public Administration Review* 1(3): 281–86.

Marková, Ivana. 2005. *Insight in Psychiatry*. Cambridge: Cambridge University Press.

Mason, Paul (ed.). 2003. *Criminal Visions: Media Representations of Crime and Justice*. Devon, UK: Willan Publications.

Maudsley, Henry. 1867. *The Physiology and Pathology of Mind*. New York: D. Appleton and Company.

———. 1872. *Body and Mind: An Inquiry into their Connections and Mutual Influence Especially in Connection to Mental Disorders*. New York: D. Appleton and Co.

———. 1874. *Responsibility in Mental Disease*. London: Henry S. King and Company.

Maurutto, Paula, and Kelly Hannah-Moffat. 2006. "Assembling Risk and the Restructuring of Penal Control." *British Journal of Criminology* 46: 438–54.

Mazzetti, Mark. 2010. "U.S. Is Still Using Private Spy Ring, Despite Doubts."*New York Times*, May 15, 2010. Accessed from www.nytimes.com/2010/05/16/world/16contractors.html, June 30, 2010.

McLaughlin, Eugene, and Karim Murji. 2001. "Lost Connections and New Directions: Neo-Liberalism, New Public Managerialism and the 'Modernization' of the British Police." Pp. 104–21 in Kevin Stenson and Robert R. Sullivan (eds.), *Crime, Risk and Justice: The Politics of Crime Control in Liberal Democracies*. Cullompton, UK: Willan Publishing.

Meehl, Paul E. 1954. *Clinical versus Statistical Prediction*. Minneapolis: University of Minnesota Press.

Meitzen, August, and Ronald P. Falkner. 1891. "History, Theory and Technique of Statistics. Part First: The History of Statistics."*Annals of the American Academy of Political and Social Sciences* 1 (Supplement 2, Part 1): 1–100.

Meltzer, Bernard D. 1965. "Labor Unions, Collective Bargaining, and the Antitrust Laws." *University of Chicago Law Review* 32(4): 659–734.

Menzies, Robert J., Christopher Webster, and Diana Sepejak. 1985. "The Dimensions of Dangerousness: Evaluating the Accuracy of Psychometric Predictions of Violence Among Forensic Patients." *Law and Human Behavior* 9(1): 49–70.

Meyer, Adolf. 1896. "A Short Sketch of the Problem of Psychiatry." *The American Journal of Insanity*, Special Number, Vol. 53.

———. 1952 (1916). "The Psychopathic Hospital Laboratory of Social Hygiene." *The Collected Papers of Adolf Meyer, Volume IV*. Baltimore: Johns Hopkins University Press.

———. 1952 (1917). "Organization of Eugenics Investigation." *The Collected Papers of Adolf Meyer, Volume IV*. Baltimore: Johns Hopkins University Press.

Mihm, Fred P. 1954. "A Re-examination of the Validity of our Sex Psychopath Statutes in the Light of Recent Appeal Cases and Experience." *Journal of Criminal Law, Criminology and Police Science* 44(6): 716–36.

Miko, Francis T., and Christian Froehlich. 2004. "Germany's Role in Fighting Terrorism: Implications for U.S. Policy." CRS Report for Congress. Congressional Research Service. Retrieved from www.dtic.mil/cgi-bin/GetTRDoc?Location=U2&doc=GetTRDoc.pdf&AD=ADA444776, April 29, 2010.

Millon, Theodore, Erik Simonsen, and Morten Birket Smith. 1998. "Historical Conceptions of Psychopathy in the United States and Europe." Pp. 3–32 in Theodore Millon, Erik Simonsen, Roger D. Davis, and Morten Birket Smith (eds.), *Psychopathy: Antisocial, Criminal, and Violent Behavior*. New York: Guilford.

Mitchell, Don, and Lynn A. Staeheli. 2005. "Permitting Protest: Parsing the Fine Geography of Dissent in America." *International Journal of Urban and Regional Research* 29(4): 796–813.

Monahan, John. 1978. "The Prediction of Violent Criminal Behavior: A Methodological Critique and Prospectus." Pp. 244–69 in Alfred Blumstein, Jacqueline Cohen, and Daniel Nagin (eds.), *Deterrence and Incapacitation: Estimating the Effects of Criminal Sanctions on Crime Rate*. Washington, DC: National Academy of Sciences.

———. 1981. *Predicting Violent Behavior: An Assessment of Clinical Techniques*. Beverly Hills, CA: Sage.

Monahan, John, and Henry Steadman. 1996. *Violence and Mental Disorder: Developments in Risk Assessment*. Chicago: University of Chicago Press.

Monahan, John, Henry J. Steadman, Paul S. Appelbaum, Pamela C. Robbins, Edward P. Mulvey, Eric Silver, Loren H. Roth, and Thomas Grisso. 2000. "Developing a Clinically Useful Actuarial Tool for Assessing Violence Risk." *British Journal of Psychiatry* 176: 312–19.

Monahan, John, Henry J. Steadman, Eric Silver, Paul S. Appelbaum, Pamela C. Robbins, Edward P. Mulvey, Loren H. Roth, Thomas Grisso, and Steven Banks. 2001. *Rethinking Risk Assessment: The MacArthur Study of Mental Disorder and Violence*. Oxford: Oxford University Press.

Monahan, Torin (ed.). 2006. *Surveillance and Security: Technological Politics and Power in Everyday Life*. New York: Routledge.

Morris, Norval. 1974. *The Future of Imprisonment*. Chicago: University of Chicago Press.

Morris, Norval, and Marc Miller. 1985. "Predictions of Dangerousness." *Crime and Justice* 6: 1–50.

Morrison, W. D. 1892. "The Study of Crime." *Mind* (New Series) 1(4): 489–517.

Murray, Robert K. 1955. *Red Scare: A Study in National Hysteria, 1919–1920*. Minneapolis: University of Minnesota Press.

Nanes, Susan R. 2005. "'The Constitutional Infringement Zone': Protest Pens and Demonstration Zones at the 2004 National Political Conventions." *Louisiana Law Review* 66(1): 189–232.

Norwood, Stephen H. 2001. *Strikebreaking and Intimidation: Mercenaries and Masculinity in Twentieth-Century America*. Chapel Hill: University of North Carolina Press.

Oehmichen, Anna. 2008. "Incommunicado Detention in Germany: An Example of Reactive Anti-terror Legislation and Long-term Consequences." *German Law Journal* 9(7): 855–87.

Olson, Harry. 1925. "Crime and Heredity." *Research Studies of Crime as Related to Heredity*. Chicago: Municipal Court of Chicago.

O'Malley, Pat. 1992. "Risk, Power and Crime Prevention." *Economy and Society* 21(3): 252–75.

———. 2000. "Risk Societies and the Government of Crime." Pp. 17–33 in Mark Brown and John Pratt (eds.), *Dangerous Offender: Punishment and Social Order*. New York: Routledge.

———. 2002. "Globalising Risk? Distinguishing Styles of 'Neo-Liberal' Criminal Justice in Australia and the USA." *Criminology and Criminal Justice* 2(2): 205–22.

———. 2004. *Risk, Uncertainty, Government*. London: Glasshouse Press.

Orren, Karen. 1991. *Belated Feudalism: Labor, the Law, and Liberal Development in the United States*. Cambridge: Cambridge University Press.

Overholser, Winfred. 1932. "Two Years' (1928–1930) Experience with the Briggs Law in Massachusetts." *Journal of Criminal Law and Criminology* 23(3): 415–26.
———. 1934. "Briggs Law of Massachusetts: A Review and an Appraisal." *American Journal of Psychiatry* 91: 585–91.
Papke, David Ray. 1999. *The Pullman Case: The Clash of Labor and Capital in Industrial America*. Lawrence: University Press of Kansas.
Parmalee, Maurice. 1908. *The Principles of Anthropology and Sociology in Their Relations to Criminal Procedure*. New York: Macmillan.
Partridge, G. E. 1930. "Current Conceptions of Psychopathic Personality." *American Journal of Psychiatry* 87: 53–99.
Pasquino, Pascale. 1991. "Theatricum Politicum: The Genealogy of Capital-Police and the State of Prosperity." Pp. 105–18 in Graham Burchell, Colin Gordon, and Peter Miller (eds.), *The Foucault Effect: Studies in Governmentality*. Chicago: University of Chicago Press.
Pearson, Karl. 1901. *National Life from the Standpoint of Science: An Address Delivered at Newcastle*. London: Adam and Charles Black.
Penn, Everette B., George E. Higgins, Shaun L. Gabbidon, and Kareem L. Jordan. 2009. "Governmental Efforts on Homeland Security and Crime: Public Views and Opinions." *American Journal of Criminal Justice* 34: 28–40.
Petrunik, Michael. 1982. "The Politics of Dangerousness." *International Journal of Law and Psychiatry* 5: 225–53.
Pfohl, Stephen. 1978. *Predicting Dangerousness: The Social Construction of Psychiatric Reality*. Lexington, MA: D. C. Heath and Company.
Ploscowe, Morris. 1960. "Sex Offenses: The American Legal Context." *Law and Contemporary Problems* 25(2): 217–24.
Poovey, Mary. 1998. *The History of the Modern Fact: Problems of Knowledge in the Sciences of Wealth and Society*. Chicago: University of Chicago Press.
Post, Louis F. 1923. *The Deportations Delirium of Nineteen-twenty: A Personal Narrative of an Historic Official Experience*. Chicago: C. H. Kerr.
Pratt, John. 1997. *Governing the Dangerous: Dangerousness, Law and Social Change*. Sydney: Federation Press.
Preston, William. 1966. *Aliens and Dissenters*. New York: Harper and Row.
Prins, H. A. 1981. "Dangerous People or Dangerous Situations? Some Implications for Assessment and Management." *Medicine, Science and Law* 21: 121–33.
Pritchard, James Cowles. 1837. *Treatise on Insanity and Other Disorders Affecting the Mind*. Philadelphia: E. L Carey and A. Hart.
Pyle, W. H. 1912. "Mental and Physical Examination of School Children in Rural Districts." *Psychological Clinic* 6: 260–62.
Quetelet, Adolphe. 1968 (1842). *A Treatise on Man and the Development of His Faculty*. New York: Burt Franklin.
Quinsey, Vernon L., Grant T. Harris, Marnie E. Rice, and Catherine A. Cormier (1998). *Violent Offenders: Appraising and Managing Risk*. Washington, DC: American Psychological Association.
Radzinowicz, Leon. 1965. "Ideology and Crime: The Determinist Position." *Columbia Law Review* 65(6): 1047–60.
Rafter, Nicole. 1988. *White Trash: The Eugenic Family Studies, 1877–1919*. Boston: Northeastern University Press.
———. 1997a. *Creating Born Criminals*. Champagne: University of Illinois Press.
———. 1997b. "Psychopathy and the Evolution of Criminological Knowledge." *Theoretical Criminology* 1(2): 235–59.
———. 2004a. "Earnest A. Hooton and the Biological Tradition in American Criminology." *Criminology* 42 (3): 735–71.
———. 2004b. "The Unrepentant Horse-slasher: Moral Insanity and the Origins of Criminological Thought." *Criminology* 42(4): 977–1006.
Ray, Issac. 1871. *Treatise on the Medical Jurisprudence of Insanity*. Boston: Little, Brown and Company.

Reichman, Nancy. 1986. "Managing Crime Risks: Toward an Insurance Based Model of Social Control." Pp. 151–72 in Steven Spitzer and Andrew T. Scull (eds.), *Research in Law, Deviance and Social Control, Vol. 8*. Greenwich, CT: JAI Press.

Reilly, Philip R. 1991. *The Surgical Solution: The History of Involuntary Sterilization in the US*. Baltimore/London: Johns Hopkins University Press.

Reinarman, Craig, and Harry G. Levine. 1997. *Crack in America: Demon Drugs and Social Justice*. Berkeley, CA: University of California Press.

Reiner, Robert, Sonia Livingstone, and Jessica Allen. 2000. "No More Happy Endings: Media and Popular Concern about Crime since the Second World War." Pp. 107–25 in Tim Hope and Richard Sparks (eds.), *Crime, Risk and Insecurity: Law and Order in Everyday Life and Political Discourse*. London/New York: Routledge.

Reinhardt, James M., and Edward C. Fisher. 1949. "The Sexual Psychopath and the Law." *Journal of Criminal Law and Criminology* 39(6): 734–42.

Rennie, Ysabel F. 1978. *The Search for Criminal Man: A Conceptual History of the Dangerous Offender*. Lexington, MA: Lexington Books.

Ribot, T. H. 1891. *Heredity: A Psychological Study of its Phenomena, Laws, Causes, and Consequences*. New York: D. Appleton and Company.

———. 1906 (1884). *Disease of the Personality*. Chicago: Open Court Publishing Company.

Rigakos, George S., and Richard W. Hadden. 2001. "Crime, Capitalism and the 'Risk Society': Towards the Same Olde Modernity?" *Theoretical Criminology* 5(1): 61–84.

Risen, James, and Eric Lichtblau (2005). "Bush Lets U.S. Spy on Callers Without Courts." *New York Times*, December 16, 2005.

Robinson, Louis N. 1933. "Institutions for Defective Delinquents." *Journal of Criminal Law and Criminology* 24(2): 352–99.

Rose, Henry. 1962. "A Critical Look at the Hatch Act." *Harvard Law Review* 75(3): 510–26.

Rosenfeld, Richard. 2004. "Terrorism and Criminology." Pp. 19–32 in Matthew Deflem (ed.), *Terrorism and Counter-Terrorism: Criminological Perspectives*. Amsterdam: Elsevier.

Ross, Dorothy. 1984. "Social Science and the Idea of Progress." In Thomas L. Haskell (ed.), *Authority of Experts: Studies in History and Theory*. Bloomington: Indiana University Press.

Ross, Edward. 1901. *Social Control: A Survey of the Foundations of Order*. New York: Macmillan Company.

Rule, James B., Douglas McAdam, Linda Stearns, and David Aglow. 1983. "Documentary Identification and Mass Surveillance in the United States." *Social Problems* 31(2): 222–34.

Rush, Benjamin. 1830. *Diseases of the Mind*. Philadelphia: John Grigg.

Salekin, R. T., R. Rogers, and K. W. Sewell. 1996. "A Review and Meta-analysis of the Psychopathy Checklist and Psychopathy Checklist—Revised: Predictive Validity of Dangerousness." *Clinical Psychology: Science and Practice* 3: 203–15.

Sarbin, Thomas R. 1944. "Clinical Psychology—Art or Science?" *Psychometrika* 6: 391–400.

Sasson, Theodore. 2000. "Willie Horton's Long Shadow: Punitiveness and Managerialism in Massachusetts Penal Policy, 1988–1999." Pp. 228–51 in Tim Hope and Richard Sparks (eds.), *Crime, Risk and Insecurity: Law and Order in Everyday Life and Political Discourse*. London/New York: Routledge.

Schumpeter, Joseph. 1942. *Capitalism, Socialism and Democracy*. New York: Harper and Row.

Shah, Salim A. 1981. "Dangerousness: Conceptual, Prediction and Public Policy Issues." Pp. 151–78 in J. Ray Hays, Thomm Kevin Roberts, Kenneth S. Solway, et al. (eds.), *Violence and the Violent Individual*. New York: S. P. Medical and Scientific Books.

Shearing, Clifford D., and Phillip C. Stenning. 1997. "From the Panopticon to Disney World: The Development of Discipline." Pp. 300–304 in Ronald V. Clarke (ed.),

Situational Crime Prevention: Successful Case Studies. Monsey, NY: Criminal Justice Press.

Silver, Eric, William R. Smith, and Steven Banks. 2000. "Constructing Actuarial Devices for Predicting Recidivism: A Comparison of Methods." *Criminal Justice and Behavior* 27: 733–64.

Simon, Jonathan. 1998. "Managing the Monstrous: Sex Offenders and the New Penology." *Psychology, Public Policy and Law* 4(1–2): 452–67.

———. 2005a. "The Reversal of Fortune: The Resurgence of Individual Risk Assessment in Criminal Justice." *Annual Review of Law and Social Sciences* 1: 397–421.

———. 2005b. *Governing through Crime: How the War on Crime transformed American Democracy and Created a Culture of Fear*. Oxford: Oxford University Press.

Skeem, Jennifer, and David Cooke. 2010. "Is Criminal Behavior a Central Component of Psychopathy? Conceptual Directions for Resolving the Debate." *Psychological Assessment* 22(2): 433–45.

Slobogin, Christopher. 1984. "Dangerousness and Expertise." *University of Pennsylvania Law Review* 133(1): 97–174.

———. 2006 . "Dangerousness and Expertise Redux." *Emory Law Journal* 56(2): 275–325.

Smelser, Marshall. 1954. "George Washington and the Alien and Sedition Acts." *American Historical Review* 59(2): 322–34.

Smith, J. David. 1985. *Minds Made Feeble: The Myth and Legacy of the Kallikaks*. Rockville, MD: Aspen Systems Corporation.

Smith, James Morton. 1954. "The Enforcement of the Alien Friends Act of 1798." *The Mississippi Valley Historical Review* 41(1): 85–104.

Smith, Jessie Spaulding. 1914. "Marriage, Sterilization and Commitment Laws Aimed at Decreasing Mental Deficiency." *Journal of the American Institute of Criminal Law and Criminology* 5(3): 364–70.

Smith, Robert Michael. 2003. *From Blackjacks to Briefcases: A History of Commercialized Strikebreaking and Unionbusting in the United States*. Athens: Ohio University Press.

Sombart, Werner. 1915. *The Quintessence of Capitalism: A Study of the History and Psychology of the Modern Business Man* (trans. M. Epstein). New York: E. P. Dutton and Company.

Sparks, Richard. 1992. *Television and the Drama of Crime: Moral Tales and the Place of Crime in Public Life*. Buckingham, UK: Open University Press.

Spaulding, Edith R. 1915. "The Results of Mental and Physical Examinations of Four Hundred Women Offenders—With Particular Reference to Their Treatment during Commitment." *Journal of the American Institute of Criminal Law and Criminology* 5(5): 704–17.

———. 1923. *An Experimental Study of Psychopathic Delinquent Women*. Patterson, NJ: Montclair Smith.

Spaulding, Edith, and William Healy. 1914. "Inheritance as a Factor in Criminality: A Study of a Thousand Cases of Young Repeated Offenders." *Bulletin of the American Academy of Medicine Vol. XV* (February 1914).

SSCSGORIA. 1976. Senate Select Committee to Study Governmental Operations with Respect to Intelligence Activities: Supplementary Detailed Staff Reports on Intelligence Activities and Rights of Americans. Accessed from www.icdc.com/~paulwolf/cointelpro/churchfinalreportIIIj.htm, April 24, 2010.

Stanco, Elizabeth. 2000. "Victims 'R US: The Life History of 'Fear of Crime' and the Politicisation of Violence." Pp. 13–30 in Tim Hope and Richard Sparks (eds.), *Crime, Risk and Insecurity: Law and Order in Everyday Life and Political Discourse*. London/New York: Routledge.

Staples, William G. 1998. *The Culture of Surveillance: Discipline and Social Control in the United States*. New York: St. Martin's Press.

Steadman, Henry. 1973. "Follow-Up on *Baxstrom* Patients Returned to Hospitals for the Criminally Insane." *American Journal of Psychiatry* 130 (3): 317–19.

———. 1976. "Predicting Dangerousness." In D. J. Madden and J. R. Lion (eds.), *Rage, Hate: Assault and Other Forms of Violence*. New York: Spectrum.
Steadman, Henry J., and Joseph J. Cocozza. 1974. *Careers of the Criminally Insane*. Lexington, MA: Lexington Books.
———. 1978. "Selective Reporting and the Public's Misconceptions of the Criminally Insane." *Public Opinion Quarterly* 41(4): 523–33.
Steadman, Henry J., Eric Silver, John Monahan, Paul S. Appelbaum, Pamela C. Robbins, Edward P. Mulvey, Thomas Grisso, Loren H. Roth, and Steven Banks. 2000. "A Classification Tree Approach to the Development of Actuarial Violence Risk Assessment Tools." *Law and Human Behavior* 24: 83–100.
Stenson, Kevin. 2001. "The New Politics of Crime Control." Pp. 15–28 in Kevin Stenson and Robert R. Sullivan (eds.), *Crime, Risk and Justice: The Politics of Crime Control in Liberal Democracies*. Cullompton, UK: Willan Publishing.
Stenson, Kevin, and Adam Edwards. 2001. "Crime Control and Liberal Government: The 'Third Way' and the Return to the Local." Pp. 68–86 Kevin Stenson and Robert R. Sullivan (eds.), *Crime, Risk and Justice: The Politics of Crime Control in Liberal Democracies*. Cullompton, UK: Willan Publishing.
Stevenson, Jonathan. 2003. "How Europe and America Defend Themselves." *Foreign Affairs* 82(2): 75–90.
Stone, Alan A. 1976. "The Tarasoff Decisions: Suing Psychotherapists to Safeguard Society." *Harvard Law Review* 90(2): 358–78.
Stone, Geoffrey R. 2004. *Perilous Times: Free Speech in Wartime from the Sedition Act of 1798 to the War on Terrorism*. New York: W. W. Norton & Company.
Stromquist, Shelton A. 1987. *Generation of Boomers: The Pattern of Railroad Labor Conflict in Nineteenth-Century America*. Urbana: University of Illinois Press.
Strum, Philippa. 1993. *Brandeis: Beyond Progressivism*. Lawrence: University Press of Kansas.
Sullivan, Robert R. 2001. "The Schizophrenic State: Neo-liberal Criminal Justice." Pp. 29–47 in Kevin Stenson and Robert R. Sullivan (eds.), *Crime, Risk and Justice: The Politics of Crime Control in Liberal Democracies*. Cullompton, UK: Willan Publishing.
Sutherland, Edwin. 1950. "The Sexual Psychopath Laws." *Journal of Criminal Law and Criminology* 40(5): 543–54.
Szasz, Thomas. 1961. *The Myth of Mental Illness*. New York: Hoeber.
———. 1988. *Schizophrenia: The Sacred Symbol of Psychiatry*. Syracuse, NY: Syracuse University Press.
Talbert, Roy. 1991. *Negative Intelligence: The Army and the American Left, 1917–1941*. Jackson: University of Mississippi Press.
Terman, Lewis. 1916a. *The Measurement of Intelligence: An Explanation of and a Complete Guide for the Use of the Stanford Revision and Extension of the Binet-Simon Intelligence Scale*. Boston/New York: Houghton Mifflin Company.
———. 1916b. "The Binet Scale and the Diagnosis of Feeblemindedness." *Journal of the American Institute of Criminal Law and Criminology* 7(4): 530–43.
Thayer, Walter N. 1925. "The Criminal and the Napanoch Plan." *Journal of American Institute of Criminal Law and Criminology* 16(2): 278–89.
Theoharis, Athan. 1978a. *Spying on Americans: Political Surveillance from Hoover to the Huston Plan*. Philadelphia: Temple University Press.
———. 1978b. "The Truman Administration and the Decline of Civil Liberties: The FBI's Success in Securing Authorization for a Preventive Detention Program." *Journal of American History* 64(4): 1010–30.
Thornberry, Terence P., and Joseph E. Jacoby. 1979. *The Criminally Insane: A Community Follow-up of Mentally Ill Offenders*. Chicago: University of Chicago Press.
Thornton, Nathaniel. 1951. "The Relationship between Crime and Psychopathology." *Journal of Criminal Law, Criminology and Police Science* 42(2): 199–204.
Tirman, John. 2004. *The Maze of Fear: Migration and Security after September 11*. New York: New Press.

Tomlins, Christopher. 1993. *Law, Labor, and Ideology in the Early American Republic*. Cambridge: Cambridge University Press.
Trent, James W. 1995. *Inventing the Feeble Mind: A History of Mental Retardation in the United States*. Berkeley: University of California Press.
Tsoukala, Anastassia. 2006. "Democracy in the Light of Security: British and French Political Discourses on Domestic Counter-Terrorism Policies." *Political Studies* 54: 607–27.
Tumlin, Karen C. 2004. "Suspect First: How Terrorism Policy is Reshaping Immigration Policy." *California Law Review* 92(4): 1173–1240.
U.S. Supreme Court. 1966. *Baxstrom v. Herold,* 383 U.S. 107 (1966).
———.1967. *United States v. Robel,* 389 U.S. 258 (1967).
———. 1972. *Johnson v. Indiana,* 406 U.S. 715 (1972).
———. 1979. *Addington V. Texas,* 441 U.S. 418 (1979).
Van Zuylen, Marina. 2005. *Monomania*. Ithaca, NY: Cornell University Press.
Verplaetse, Jan. 2002. "Prosper Despine's *Psychologie naturelle* and the Discovery of the Remorseless Criminal in Nineteenth-century France." *History of Psychiatry* 13(50): 153–75.
Wacquant, Loic. 2008. *The Urban Outcasts: The Comparative Sociology of Advanced Marginality*. Cambridge: Polity Press.
Walklate, Sandra. 2001. "Fearful Communities?" *Urban Studies* 36: 929–40.
Wallin, J. E. W. 1913. "Re-averments Respecting Psycho-clinical Norms and Scales of Development." *Psychological Clinic* 7: 89–96.
Warren, Carol A. B. 1979. "The Social Construction of Dangerousness."*Urban Life* 8: 359–84.
Washington Post. 2007. "FBI Sought Authority To Detain Thousands: Declassified Papers Detail Hoover Plan During Korean War." December 23, 2007. Accessed from www.washingtonpost.com/wp-dyn/content/article/2007/12/22/ AR2007122201487.html, January 31, 2010.
Weber, Max. 2007 (1927). *General Economic History*. New York: Cosimo.
Webster, Christopher. 1998. "Comment on Thomas Mathieson's Selective Incapacitation Revisited." *Law and Human Behavior* 22: 471–76.
Webster, Christopher D., Derek Eaves, Kevin S. Douglas, and Anne M. Wintrup. 1995. *The HCR-20 Scheme: The Assessment of Dangerousness and Risk*. Vancouver, Canada: Simon Fraser University and British Columbia Forensic Psychiatric Services Commission.
Webster, Christopher, Robert J. Menzies, and Margaret A. Jackson. 1982. *Clinical Assessment Before Trial: Legal Issues and Mental Disorder*. Toronto: Butterworths.
Weindling, Paul. J. 2005. *Nazi Medicine and the Nuremberg Trials: From Medical War Crimes to Informed Consent*. New York: Palgrave Macmillan.
Wenk, Ernest A., James O. Robison, and Gerald W. Smith. 1972. "Can Violence Be Predicted?" *Crime and Delinquency* 18(4): 393–402.
Wetzell, Richard F. 2000. *Inventing the Criminal: A History of German Criminology, 1880–1945*. Durham: University of North Carolina Press.
Wiecek, William M. 2001. "The Legal Foundations of Domestic Anticommunism: The Background of *Dennis v United States*." *Supreme Court Review* Vol. 2001: 375–434.
Wilbur, H. B. 1877. "The Classification of Idiocy." *Proceedings of the Association of Medical Officers of Hospitals and Asylums*.
Wile, Ira S. 1939. "Mental Tests and the Marriage Law." *Living: Journal of the National Council of Family Relations* 1(4): 78–79.
Williams, David. 1981. "The Bureau of Investigation and Its Critics, 1919-1921: The Origins of Federal Political Surveillance." *Journal of American History* 68(3): 560–79.
Willrich, Michael. 1998. "The Two Percent Solution: Eugenic Jurisprudence and the Socialization of American Law, 1900–1930." *Law and History Review* 16(1): 63–111.
———. 2003. *City of Courts: Socializing Justice in Progressive Era Chicago*. Cambridge: Cambridge University Press.

Wilson, James Q. 1995. "Crime and Public Policy." Pp. 489–510 in James Q. Wilson and Joan Petersilia (eds.), *Crime*. San Francisco: ICS Press.

Woodbury, Frank. 1913. "Benjamin Rush: Patriot, Physician and Psychiater: A Centennial Memorial Note." Pp. 427–30 in *Proceedings of the American Medico-psychological Association*. Baltimore: Lord Baltimore Press.

Wong, Katherine. 2006. "The NSA Terrorist Surveillance Program." *Harvard Journal of Legislation* 43(2): 517–34.

Yerkes, Robert M. 1916. "Mental Examination of Police and Court Cases." *Journal of the American Institute of Criminal Law and Criminology* 7(3): 366–72.

———. 1943. *Chimpanzees: A Laboratory Colony*. New York: Johnson Reprint Corporation.

Yerkes, Robert M., James W. Bridges, and Rose S. Hardwick. 1915. *A Point Scale for Measuring Mental Ability*. Baltimore: Warwick and York.

Young, Jock. 1999. *The Exclusive Society: Social Exclusion, Crime and Difference in Late Modernity*. London: Sage.

Zenderland, Leila. 1998. *Measuring Minds: Henry Herbert Goddard and the Origins of American Intelligence Testing*. New York: Cambridge University Press.

Zinn, Howard. 1980. *A People's History of the United States*. New York: Harper & Row.

Index

www.ingramcontent.com/pod-product-compliance
Ingram Content Group UK Ltd.
Pitfield, Milton Keynes, MK11 3LW, UK
UKHW041122071026
15587UKWH00009B/88